Duty to Deliberate

Justice by Chance or by Design?

A Novel

Kausalya Hegde

COPYRIGHT NOTICE

Copyright © 2021, Kausalya M. Hegde. All Rights Reserved. No part of this publication may be reproduced, stored in a retrieval system, stored in a database and/or published by any means, whether electronic, mechanical, manual, photocopying, recording or otherwise, without the express written permission of the author. To obtain permission to copy, email contact@hegdekesq.com

Published in 2023
by ***HeGdE*** PublishinG CA 94588

DISCLAIMERS

This is a work of fiction. Names, characters, places and events are products of author's imagination or used fictitiously and resemblance to actual events, locales or people is entirely coincidental.

Some real events, precedents, cases, institutions, public offices, etc., are used fictitiously. NOTHING in this book is claimed as binding on any courts or regulatory authorities in any jurisdiction. NOTHING in this book should be taken as legal advice.

For Sri Hari

CONTENTS:

- TITLE PAGE I
- COPYRIGHT NOTICE II
- DISCLAIMERS II
- 1. TRANSMUTED COURTS 9
- 2. LEGAL ASSISTANCE 17
- 3. REASONED DECISIONS 29
- 4. NEW HORIZONS 34
- 5. THE NEWS 39
- 6. UNFAIR ADVANTAGE 43
- 7. NARROW ESCAPE 55
- 8. UNSEEN JUSTICE 66
- 9. NEW WORLD 72
- 10. CONFLUENCE 85
- 11. THE BOX 97
- 12. DICEY JUSTICE........................... 108
- 13. NULLIFICATION 118
- 14. THE MAGNA CARTA 130
- 15. THE TEST 140
- 16. SHARING TIME 150

17. VARIED VIEWS 158
18. PRO BONO COUNSEL 166
19. CONTEMPLATION 172
20. MAJOR DECISION 178
21. INTEGRITY 189
22. INNOCENT INDIGENT 199
23. THE SPY 202
24. TRANSFORMATION 211
25. PLEA BARGAIN 220
26. VOIR DIRE 227
27. ENTROPY 230
28. STORMY SEMINAR 242
29. INCONGRUITY 252
30. CRUSADER 258
31. PEERS FOR PEERS 267
32. GOOD JUDGMENT 274
33. UNFORESEEN 281
34. EVALUATION 287
35: MAJOR HURDLE 295
36. HIGH STAKES 307

37. REVIEW PETITION 316

38. HEARING 323

39. COUNTER 333

40. UNRELENTING.............................345

41. ACQUIESCENCE 351

42. A FAIR BALANCE 361

43. FORUM BUFFET..........................373

44. THE TRIAL 381

45. CRUCIAL TESTIMONY 394

46. FINAL ARGUMENTS 400

47. VERIFIED VERDICT 404

48. PEOPLE'S COURT 413

GLOSSARY 418

AUTHOR BIO......................................421

Due Deliberations…

1. Transmuted Courts

Anwitha hit the brakes as a bicyclist on the pavement swerved right in front of her car. Several vehicles came to a screeching halt behind her and some of them honked.

"Sorry sorry," said the bicyclist and rode across the street causing all the commuters to stop for him along the way. Many of them yelled simultaneously in different languages.

"Buddi ilvenayya?!" "Hey Bhagvan!" "Paithiyama?!" "Yemi idi!" "What the…Bengloor traffic hingene!"

Anwitha tried to remain calm and resumed driving when the road became clear. It was a very important day for her as a young advocate and she had stayed up till 1:00 a.m. the previous night preparing for a case.

She stopped again as the lights turned red at a traffic signal on Cubbon Road. Though it was early morning, this part of the city of Bangalore was already busy with traffic. She had skipped breakfast and left the house at

7:30 a.m. to avoid being late that day but not without offering special prayers to Ganesha, the remover of all obstacles.

It began to drizzle.

"Oh, the first rains of 2007!" she quickly raised the window glass all the way up just as the pleasant earthy smell filled the air. *"About time as it is the end of June already."*

She picked up her thermos, sipped the hot masala tea and relaxed watching the little rain drops fall on the windshield. Anwitha was in her mid twenties, five feet five inches tall, slim and of wheatish complexion. She had a round face, large brown eyes, small nose, oval mouth and had rolled up her shoulder length black wavy hair in a bun to look more mature.

She looked through the window to her left. Despite the rain, a few laborers were walking on the pavement, carrying decorating items to prepare for the upcoming celebrations of the Independence Day at Parade Grounds. Decades ago, that entire area around Parade Grounds was controlled by the British Raj, where they had their largest military cantonment in southern India and the rest of the city was ruled by the Mysore Kingdom. The British brought with them the English common law which eventually replaced the traditional forms of dispute resolution like mediation and arbitration in the country. Worldwide lately, these methods were being recommended as faster alternatives to resolve disputes.

"Actually, common law litigation used to be the alternative introduced in India by the British," Anwitha set the empty thermos aside. *"We had Panchayats, Adhyakshas and the King's court back then."*

The traffic lights turned green. Anwitha continued driving on Cubbon Road for a while and then turned left to enter into the Cubbon Park to reach the rear parking lot of the Karnataka High Court premises. The rains stopped just as she parked her compact car in her favorite spot which was closest to the High Court building's rear entrance. It was 8: 40 a.m.

"It took me over an hour to get here despite starting so early," she thought getting out of the car.

She stared at the red building in front of her. The stone and brick structure in Graeco-Roman style of architecture stretched across several meters. It had rows of arches along its expansive width, supported by pillars and columns. In the center and at the two ends of the building were ionic porticos and above each portico was a terrace with a pediment held up by huge cylindrical columns.

Although she'd been coming to work here every day for almost a year now, it felt different today. She looked at the Indian national flag fluttering on top of the building. She read the inscriptions on the architrave, both in her mother tongue Kannada and in English, 'Karnataka Uchcha Nyayalaya…The High Court of Karnataka'. She felt excitement and nervousness at the same time.

"Hope nothing goes wrong today," she prayed. She picked up her black coat and the advocate robe from the back seat of her car and wore them. She put the lawyer's band in her coat pocket.

"The lot will be full by 9 a.m., glad I got here early," she thought looking around and walked towards the building's rear entrance.

"I'll come back for my files later, I need to eat first," she climbed up the steps and entered the vestibule.

The lobby opened onto the main corridor of that floor. She stepped into the long corridor with rows of court halls on the left, overlooking the parking lot on the right. The court halls were not yet open. On reaching the stairs leading to the canteen on the upper floor, she held up the pleats of her saree to avoid tripping on the long fabric. Saree was considered as one of the more formal attires for women lawyers and it went very well with her lawyer's attire, the black coat and the robe.

As she entered the canteen on the front terrace, the aroma of food made her realize how hungry she was. She ordered a plate of idly sambar.

There were two senior male advocates in one corner, tactfully holding little steel cups of steaming beverage and discussing something. One of them acknowledged Anwitha and continued his discussion with his friend, "Did you hear about the case of two surgeons in…"

"Tagolli madam," the canteen guy handed Anwitha a steel plate of steaming idlies and sambar.

She smiled, took the plate and went to the front edge of the terrace and began eating, enjoying the view of the majestic Vidhana Soudha across the street which was the seat of the bicameral legislature of the State of Karnataka.

When she finished her breakfast, the front parking lot was almost full and the court premises began to get noisier.

"It's 9:40 a.m.," she wore the lawyer's band and walked back to her car. It was now hot and sunny.

She removed a large bag containing her file and books from the boot. When commuting by her scooty before, carrying all of those things needed a lot of creative thinking.

The doors of the court halls all along the corridors were now open. Anwitha carried the bag to court hall 6, took her case file and books out of it. She placed the books on the right front desk on its far left side. Within the enclosure right before the raised seat of the Judge, the bench clerk was busy organizing his stuff.

"Good morning Anwitha madam," he smiled.

"Good morning," she smiled back.

"Your case is listed for final hearing today."

"Yes."

"Are you going to argue it or your senior?"

"I am,"

"Best of luck madam!"

"Thanks! It is my first final hearing argument in High Court. During the last one year I've been appearing only in admission cases."

"Hmm. I know you'll do well."

"Thank you! I hope so too," she sat down in the second row.

The court hall was soon full with advocates. Mr. Venkat, a designated senior counsel for the opposing side in Anwitha's case walked in and sat beside her.

Promptly, at 10:30 a.m., Justice Raghu arrived. He was known to be a tough Judge and intolerant of unprepared counselors. Everyone stood up as the Judge entered. After the Judge sat down, the bench clerk began calling out the cases.

Mr. Venkat leaned towards Anwitha and asked in a low voice, "Are you doing this hearing today or are you asking for an adjournment?"

"I'm going to argue this today," she said.

"Oh, okay,"

Fifteen minutes of admission matters later, Anwitha's case was called. She went forward to the right front desk, pulled the portable lectern adjacent to her books and placed her file on the lectern.

"Appearing for the petitioner your lordship," she opened the file and took her notes out.

The respondent's counsel Mr. Venkat along with his assistant lawyer went to the left front desk and grabbed his lectern.

"For the respondent your lordship," he said.

The bench clerk handed the court copy of the case file to the Judge. The Judge opened the file and took out his notes. He looked at Anwitha and said, "Okay. Tell me the facts of the case ma'm!"

2. Legal Assistance

Anwitha said, "I was dismissed from service after a departmental inquiry. The main grounds against the dismissal order passed by the quasi judicial authority are,"

The Judge nodded. Anwitha looked at her notes.

"I…," a lot of lawyers would submit in first person while representing their clients before a Judge, and Anwitha preferred that style too, rather than referring to her clients as "my client".

"had requested for representation by a lawyer during the departmental enquiry, but it was denied by the employer. A representation by a co-worker was given instead. The co-worker was experienced in other types of matters, but this particular case required lawyer representation to render the representation effective or meaningul."

"Why do you say so?"

"For several reasons your lordship. First, the charges leveled were serious. If proved, they would lead to the penalty of dismissal from services. Secondly, the case involved examination of hundreds of documents. Annexures A1 to S140 from pages 59 to 300, and a large number of witnesses. Sixty seven, to be exact. Thirdly, the case involved complex issues, justifying a legal professional's help…"

She paused for a second and continued after ensuring the Judge had no trouble following what she was submitting.

"…Fourth, the only co-worker experienced in matters like this was unavailable,"

Justice Raghu nodded his head and made a note in his file.

Anwitha paused again, to see if the Judge had any question and continued, "The co-worker who represented me had no experience in dismissal matters."

"What were the charges against you?" asked the Judge.

"Demanding and taking bribe in the matter of appointment and promotion…"

"Hmm, it was a departmental enquiry. Not criminal proceedings. Peer assistance was your only right. Not lawyer representation?"

"The rules for departmental enquiry provide for lawyer representation in appropriate cases. These rules are framed by the respondent themselves,"

"What do you say Mr. Venkat?" the Judge asked turning to the respondent's lawyer.

"The petitioner was given adequate representation by the co-worker my lord…"

"How many cases has the co-worker represented before?"

"About fifteen,"

"What were the suggested penalties in those cases?"

"Stoppage of increments."

"No case involving charges incurring the penalty of dismissal?"

"No, your lordship."

"Hmmm," the Judge was quiet for a moment.

Then he asked, "Tell me Mr. Venkat, if you don't provide legal representation in a case where you propose to terminate employment, then in what case would you provide legal representation to an employee facing an inquiry?"

"Since, in an employment law case, dismissal order is the most severe penalty that can be imposed," Anwitha thought.

Senior advocate Mr. Venkat seemed to expect that question from the Judge. Knowing full well he could not justify his client's stance, he wasted no time in saying,

"We can hold a *de novo* enquiry and provide legal representation to the petitioner."

The Judge smiled. Probably he had expected that response as well.

Anwitha was fully prepared to oppose a fresh de novo enquiry against her client but waited for the Judge's response. She had seen in the last one year how Justice Raghu never failed to see beyond what the lawyers actually told him, thanks to the years of experience he had.

The Judge asked Anwitha, "When was the petitioner charged?"

Although usually he would continue with the respondent's counsel, he deliberately put questions to Anwitha as the Judge wanted to be encouraging to the young lawyer arguing her first hearing matter in the highest court of the state.

Anwitha referred to her notes and said, "Fifteen years ago."

The Judge turned to page one of the writ petition and looked at the age of the petitioner. It said fifty nine years old, and the writ petition was filed six years ago.

Justice Raghu let out a sigh. He usually did that when he had kind of made up his mind on what order to pass. Anwitha became a bit anxious.

"Where is the dismissal order ma'm?" he asked.

"Annexure S-38, my lord."

"Was there a provision for internal appeal?"

"Yes. Appeal was filed and dismissed. It is produced as annexure S-39."

The Judge began dictating the order to the stenographer.

"Orders at Annexures S-38 and 39, the order of dismissal and the order by the appellate authority respectively are hereby quashed for the reasons below…"

The Judge leaned forward as he continued.

"The matter involved serious charges against the petitioner and despite request, legal representation was denied to him during departmental enquiry. Considering the case involved examination of hundreds of documents and more than," the Judge turned toward Anwitha.

"How many witnesses ma'm?" he asked.

"Sixty seven witnesses,"

The stenographer noted it.

The Judge continued, "The representation of inexperienced co-worker did not satisfy the principles of natural justice. As the case has been long drawn for fifteen years now, and the petitioner is past the age of retirement," the Judge looked at Anwitha to confirm the fact.

Anwitha said, "Yes, your lordship."

"...the matter is not remanded back for fresh consideration or de novo enquiry. The respondent is ordered to pay full back pay with interest from the date of termination of employment to the date of retirement and full pension with interest from the date on which the petitioner would have retired...case disposed off."

The Judge put the file away for the bench clerk to pick up.

Anwitha bowed down and said, "Much obliged, your lordship."

She closed her file, picked up the books and put them in the bag and walked out of the court hall feeling completely elated. Her senior colleagues who had arrived by the time her case was called had stood and watched the Judge dictate the order. They followed her outside the court hall and congratulated her.

"Good job!" they said.

"Thanks guys!"

"I need to go get the certified copy of an order. One of you will take the files bag to office?" she asked.

"Yes. Don't worry about it."

"Thanks," she said and walked down the corridor.

She heard a voice behind her say, "Congrats ya!" Anwitha turned around and saw her buddy from kindergarten through law college walking up to her.

"I watched your arguments. You were just great!" he said.

"Thanks Sharan!"

She stopped for him to catch up to her.

Sharan was also her distant cousin and had got married recently. He was about five feet ten inches tall, lean, wheatish, had brown eyes, sharp features and was clean shaven.

"Congratulations to you and Hema, Sharan! Sorry I couldn't attend your wedding! I was really sick."

"No, I'm never going to forgive you!" said Sharan feigning anger.

"Ha ha," laughed Anwitha.

"How does it feel being a married man?"

"Great!" Sharan said. "We missed you. Everyone was there at the wedding except you!"

"Hmm, I wish I could attend too!"

"It's okay, but you should visit my wife's home town sometime. It's interesting…"

"Manapparai?"

"Yes. Nice little town. Known for its tasty murukkus and many good stuff. Now in the news because of the doctor couple case though…you must have heard?"

"What doctor couple case?!?"

"Come on Anwitha! You don't know about it?!? It's been on the news for some time now, on every channel and newspaper!"

Anwitha was embarrassed. She had no idea what he was talking about.

"Take a break ya! You don't have to work sooo hard that you become oblivious to everything else happening around you!"

"Okay, okay. Tell me now. What about that case in your wife's hometown?" said Anwitha.

"Anyways, allegedly in Manapparai, a doctor couple, both gynecologists and surgeons let their fourteen year old son perform a C-section on a pregnant woman and deliver her baby, because they hoped and wished, allegedly, according to news reports, the son could enter the Guinness book of world records for being the youngest surgeon…"

"Oh god! No!!"

"Well the mother and the baby are both fine. In fact the woman is reportedly one of their relatives and voluntarily submitted herself to the surgery by the little boy supervised by his parents."

"That is still no excuse!! It doesn't matter if the woman volunteered and was not coerced. How can someone not licensed as a doctor perform medical procedures on another human?!"

"Ya, I know, it's crazy."

They started walking towards Anwitha's car.

"So then what happened? Did the 'doctor son' make it to the Guinness book?!"

Anwitha looked up at Sharan, impatient to know what happened next.

"No no no…ha ha," Sharan laughed.

Anwitha stood half smiling, puzzled.

Sharan continued, "The parent doctors took a video footage of their son performing the surgery and proudly showed it to their colleagues. But the colleagues were horrified. Then the matter reached the concerned authorities. And the parent doctors have had their license suspended pending enquiry and criminally charged under the Indian Penal Code for endangering human life and other offenses."

"Hmm. How could they be so ignorant? They are doctors for god's sake. Didn't they know better than that? Thank god no one was actually hurt."

"Yes, considering this was not the first time the son had done this,"

"Really?!!" Anwitha shook her head in amusement and disbelief.

"Yes, when the daddy doc flaunted the video he said to his colleagues their son was pretty adept at performing C-sections and had successfully delivered babies for almost one year since he was thirteen!"

"Oh!?"

"Yes, allegedly."

"Of course allegedly. God, it is so stupid!"

"Yaa, ya," both of them laughed.

"Hmm, mathe? What else?" Sharan asked.

"Mathenilla, I have a lot of drafting work pending, need to finish it by this weekend."

They reached her car. There were several butterflies hovering over the curbside flowerbed. Looking at Anwitha staring at them, Sharan asked, "What's with you and butterflies?"

"Ah? Nothing, they are so pretty and happy,"

"Happy?! Ha ha, you are funny."

Anwitha smiled.

"Okay, got to go," she said.

"Where are you off to now?" he asked.

"To the Magistrate's court. Need to get a certified copy."

Anwitha removed her robe and put it in the car.

"How about you?" she asked.

"I'm done with my work today. Going home."

"Already?! Aha…!! Missing your new bride?"

"Told you I'm done with my work," said Sharan, feigning annoyance.

"Of course, but how did you manage that?!" Anwitha laughed.

"Aye!! Wait. I'll have my chance to tease you when you get married."

"Well, it's not going to happen for a while."

"Really!? We'll see, remember? When I was at your place to invite your parents for my wedding, they said they'll not wait for too long,"

"Well, they have to wait for some more time. At least until I'm done with my LLM."

"Oh yeah, yeah, you told me about that. Have you heard from them yet?"

"Heard from your alma mater in New York. They've offered partial scholarship. Hope WBU law school will give me full scholarship."

"Hmm. Let me know of the developments. I can help you with living arrangements over there," Sharan said grooming his hair looking in the reflection of the car window.

"Thank you Sharan."

"No problem. Bye,"

3. Reasoned Decisions

Two hours later Anwitha was back in her office. She read the copy of the order she had just got from the Magistrate's court. The client had lost in the criminal trial before the Magistrate's court and she needed to draft an appeal.

Her boss, senior advocate Mr. Srinivas, walked towards her cubicle. She stood up respectfully.

Mr. Srinivas was about sixty years old with over thirty years of law practice experience. He was known to be a thorough professional and a man of integrity, highly respected within the legal community and by his clients.

"Congrats Anwitha!" he patted her back.

"Thanks! Was a bit nervous because the court usually says peer assistance is enough in a departmental enquiry."

"Yes. Mostly it is so, but not always as you convinced the court today. It was a tough case, before a tough Judge and a tough opponent. Well done, you won your first case!" he said.

"Thank you!" Anwitha was happy her work was appreciated.

"Did you get the certified copy from the Magistrate's court?" he asked.

"Yes I did. I'm preparing the appeal."

"What are the grounds?"

"Well it appears the Judge has omitted citing reasons for some parts of the verdict…"

"Okay, And?"

"I'm also attacking some of the reasons that are cited as…bad in law?" she said, a bit diffident.

"Good, bring it to me for review when done."

"Yes,"

After Mr. Srinivas retreated to his office room, Anwitha went to the firm's library and got a couple of books to do research before drafting the appeal.

The college intern in the adjacent cubicle bent over and said, "Anwitha, can I disturb you for a minute? I had a question."

Anwitha turned towards her."No problem, what is it?"

"I overheard your discussion with senior." They all called Mr. Srinivas that.

"Why is a Judge required to give reasons for his decisions?"

"Hmmm, so that all concerned parties have a chance to verify that all relevant facts, arguments, laws and evidence have been considered and, that they were considered for the right reasons before the Judge made a decision on the case. It also helps to ascertain whether each piece of evidence was accorded proper weight," Anwitha replied, as she opened one of the books.

"Remember, we learnt in law college?" said Anwitha picking up a sticky note to bookmark a page in her book.

"That...to sustain public faith in the judiciary, justice must not only be done but must be manifestly and undoubtedly seen to be done. That's the reason for reasoned judgments," Anwitha looked at the intern and smiled.

The intern smiled back and said, "Hmm, okay. Thanks Anwitha."

"You're welcome,"

The phone on Anwitha's desk rang. She picked it up.

"Hello?"

"Hello, called your cell phone so many times!" Anwitha's mother said.

"Oh! Left it in the car probably. Yen ayitu?" Anwitha said.

The intern went to another room sensing Anwitha needed some privacy to talk.

"Can you come home a bit early today?"

"Why?"

"That boy and his family will be coming to see you. Just got a phone call from them."

"Oh no, amma, told you I'm not interested in marriage right now, also I am very busy today!"

"Please come, or your dad will be upset."

"I don't see any logic in this. Is it okay if I'm upset? For the rest of my life…?!"

"Don't argue. Just come before 7 p.m."

Anwitha was quiet.

"Hello?"

Anwitha still remained quiet.

"Are you there…?! Anwi…?!" her mom sounded anxious and angry.

Anwitha said, "Ok. But let me tell you this. I'll have to go through the whole exercise only to say no at the end of it all."

Anwitha kept the receiver down. She leaned forward, placed her elbows on the desk, and buried her face in her hands.

"This is so frustrating..."

She tried to calm herself down by breathing slowly. After a few minutes she felt better.

"I need to get away from all this."

She began to quietly draft her appeal.

4. New Horizons

Mia didn't realize that somebody was trying to get her attention. *"I need to finish this task before we land…,"* she continued reading through the file.

"Hello…would you like something to drink?"

Mia looked up at the flight attendant smiling at her.

"Yes please," she smiled back and said, "What have you got?"

"Um, we have apple juice, orange juice and…"

"I'll have some apple juice thanks!"

"Ice?"

"Yes please," Mia put the file folder in the aisle seat beside her.

"Here you are," the flight attendant handed the juice to Mia.

"Thanks," Mia grabbed the glass and took a sip of the apple juice.

"Hmm!! Cold and soothing,"

She checked the monitor in front of her to see how far she had flown.

"Okay, in about three hours I will see Logan," she mused.

While many passengers in the plane were enduring the long boring flight by sleeping through it, Mia was busy preparing a draft opening statement for a trial which needed to be ready by next morning.

"I will be with Logan but cannot really enjoy being with him until I'm done studying this thick file," she looked down at the folder beside her and took another sip of her apple juice.

Mia was five feet six inches tall, slim, had blue-green eyes, soft brown hair, small nose and high cheek bones. She grew up in Orlando, Florida in a modest family. Soon after her B.A., she got a job as a receptionist in a law firm. Few months later she became interested in studying law and enrolled in a law school. She passed the Florida Bar at the age of twenty four and continued to work in the same law firm for a while.

"By the time I land in California, I'll be totally dehydrated," she finished her apple juice, placed it in the cup holder, picked up the folder and opened the bookmarked page.

She liked working for the law firm in Orlando but wanted to be closer to her boyfriend who worked in San Francisco Bay Area. So she began applying for jobs in the west coast of USA. Luckily for her, she got an interning opportunity at the District Attorney's office in San Mateo. She was also scheduled to be interviewed a few days later for a part time job in a large law firm that had a diverse law practice in Bay Area. The recruiter had told Mia she needed to familiarize herself with California laws. Mia had taken the California Bar earlier that year and had passed in the first attempt. However, mastering many state specific laws would still take time.

***

After about two hours Mia closed the folder and put it in her backpack. *"It's done! I can email it to Mr. Peter tonight for review."*

She leaned back in her seat and looked around her. A woman sitting in the aisle seat across her was reading a thriller novel by a lawyer turned author.

"Thanks to writers like him, everyone, or at least all non-lawyers think law practice is a very glamorous profession!" Mia leaned to her left and stared down the window.

The view of the fields through the scattered bits of puffy white clouds was enchanting.

"What many do not know is, it also takes poring over loads of confusing documents, indulging in mental warfare with your opponents, day after day, week after week for years…"

While she was definitely enjoying every bit of her law practice now and feeling quite powerful with the kind of knowledge and confidence that traditional law practice gives, she disliked the long hours and overzealousness displayed by some lawyers.

"I may end up as a writer someday…who knows," she thought.

***

When she exited the San Francisco airport, it was 5 p.m. local time and pretty bright but chilly because of the strong breeze.

"Didn't think I would need it in the summer!" she quickly took out a jacket from her suitcase, put it on and called Logan.

It was picked up at one ring. "Hey!"

"Logan! Just got out of the airport."

"Okay! I'm approaching the curb side pickup area," Logan said. "There! I see you!!"

"I see you too!"

Logan parked and Mia quickly put her suitcase on the back seat of the car, hopped in and sat beside Logan.

"Hey! That was a long flight huh?" he said.

"It was okay. After having travelled to India, this didn't seem so long at all!"

"Ha ha!"

He began to drive out of the airport.

Wearing the seat belt she thought, *"I'm in a new city, new state, on the other end of the country, far from my family, know no one here except Logan! How exciting!!"*

5. The News

Anwitha noticed the draft appeal was back at her desk with some suggestions by her senior after review. She edited the draft as suggested, printed it out and signed *Anwitha Bhat* at the appropriate spots and gave it to her office clerk to be filed in court. She went back to her desk and started checking her emails on the computer.

The mood in her home was still tense after she said 'no' to the marriage proposal. Her dad would not speak to her. Her mother understood Anwitha's problem but worried her daughter might get into a lot of trouble by resisting her dad's will. Anwitha stayed in the law office for much longer that day while most of her colleagues had left for the day. Mr. Srinivas was still working. It was around 8 p.m. and very dark and raining outside. She dreaded going home but had to at some point. Working in the same city where her parents lived, she had no option but to live with them. It was an unwritten rule to live with your parents whether employed or unemployed until married. She loved them but right now the pressure from them to 'just get married' was too much for her to put up with.

"You are already too old! This is probably your last chance to get a decent, well settled boy…you are a fool to reject this proposal!" her dad had yelled at her in frustration.

"I'm only twenty five…there is no need to get all panicky. I'm just not ready yet to get married and settle down!" she had replied equally frustrated.

"Hey bhagvaan, please save me from all this conflict…," Anwitha prayed quietly, as she scrolled down the list of emails.

There it was, the answer to her prayers in the email from the West Bay University School of Law, California. Her application for the Master of Laws program for the fall of 2007 was accepted with full scholarship.

"Thank god!!" she closed her eyes and sat quietly for a few minutes.

It stopped raining.

"Okay, I better leave now,"

She shut down the computer, picked up the case files on the table and walked out of the office. As she began to drive home, she thought, *"It's late July now...I have barely enough time to wrap things up before leaving...!"*

***

When Anwitha reached home, it was 9 p.m. She rang the bell and bent her head down as she heard her mom approach the door. When her mother opened the door and let her in, she quickly rushed inside without looking up. She freshened up, changed and went over to the dining room to eat her dinner. Her parents had already eaten and were watching the late night news on TV in the living room.

She could hear the anchor on TV going, "The two doctors from Manapparai are being questioned by…"

"Oh, that must be the case Sharan was talking about," Anwitha went over to the living room.

"…it may be recalled here that this married couple, both gynecologists are facing medical malpractice charges and criminal charges for endangering human lives by allowing their fourteen year old son, to perform a C-section…the baby and the mother are both fine, but if the allegations are proved the doctor parents can have their medical licenses cancelled and…"

The photos of the doctor couple were flashed on the TV screen.

"The doctor parents are now denying that their son performed the surgery and are saying the son merely watched while they did the operation."

The anchor was now back on the screen and proceeded to another news item.

"The accused in the Jessica Lall murder case…"

Anwitha went back to finish her dinner.

6. Unfair Advantage

She ran across the long corridor praying, "Hope I can make it in time...the traffic was so bad today!"

When she reached the court hall, she paused a second to catch her breath before stepping inside nervously and bowing to the Bench.

The Judge stared at her and one of the lawyers sitting in the last row turned toward her. He said, "Madam, your case has just been dismissed!"

"What?!!" Anwitha sat up in bed, wide awake!

The clock on the side table said it was 7.30 a.m. *"Oh, thank god,"* she sighed and got out of bed.

"No time for saree draping today,"

"Tea ready. Want me to pour it in the thermos for you?" a question her mom asked every morning Anwitha went to work.

"Yes, thanks," she went to shower.

"I'll wear trousers,"

***

"There's just one case to attend to today, but I probably might end up waiting the whole day in court hall 3," Anwitha thought as she drove to the High Court.

According to the cause list for court hall 3 for that day, there were several hearing matters listed and the ones preceding hers were going to be argued by senior counsels.

"Just by sitting in the Court and observing other cases being argued we can learn so much," she thought as she entered into the High Court parking lot.

When she reached the court hall, it was in session. Anwitha bowed down as she entered the court hall and sat in a chair in the last row since her case would not be taken up soon. The division bench headed by Justice Rama Rao was an interesting court to be in. The other Judge was the recently elevated Justice Murthy who gave up a successful law practice to serve as a Judge.

Two senior advocates were on their legs and one of them was Mr. Srinivas. It appeared they had just concluded arguing a case and were exchanging pleasantries with the Judges. They were all at the same level of age and experience and enjoyed a camaraderie that's possible only among equals.

Justice Rama Rao was saying, "I know Srinivas, a lawyer's job is not easy…we Judges have our own idiosyncrasies and you need to adapt to those…we are deciding cases in different states we are asked to serve at, but we come from different parts of India, with different backgrounds, speak different native languages…"

Mr. Srinivas chuckled, "And have different 'unconscious' biases." Only someone of Mr. Srinivas's stature could have said that.

Everyone including Anwitha was curious to see what the Judges' reaction would be. The Judges began to laugh at that and everyone in the court hall joined.

Justice Rao was graceful to admit. He said, "Yes Mr. Srinivas, we are humans and can only function like humans… and it is a good thing. In fact robots are capable of complete impartiality but would they make good Judges? I think not. Only humans can appreciate human problems and emotions involved in a case and you cannot replace human Judges with machines even if it means having to deal with the side effect of some amount of bias in certain cases. "

"True," Mr. Srinivas said.

Justice Rao continued, "But the good news is, years of professional experience prior to becoming Judges will prevent us from letting any bias whether conscious or unconscious, affect our decisions…most of the times," the Judges put the case files down. The senior advocates smiled, bowed and exited the court hall.

"And also the requirement to give reasoned decisions will make a Judge aware of any unconscious bias while writing a judgment…," thought Anwitha.

The next case was called and the clerk handed the files to the Judges.

A junior advocate in his late twenties went forward with his files.

He said, "Appear for the petitioner, your lordship."

Designated senior advocate Mr. Venkat appeared for the respondent, along with his colleague who sat beside him to assist him during the arguments.

The Judges acknowledged the counsels, opened their files and began to hear the arguments.

Anwitha got up, slowly walked over to the second row and sat, to be able to better follow the arguments.

The junior advocate was extremely nervous while submitting his arguments, probably because the case was about a subject matter that was unfamiliar to him and a designated senior counsel was his opponent. They were arguing a writ appeal in an administrative law matter in which Mr. Venkat was considered an authority. The junior lawyer who was a solo practitioner routinely handled land revenue cases. Mr. Venkat was basing his arguments on a series of Supreme Court judgments, that seemed to totally favor his client.

Justice Rama Rao seemed convinced of Mr. Venkat's arguments. He turned to the junior lawyer and said, "Counselor, do you have anything more to submit?"

The junior lawyer fumbling through his file said, "No your lordship," he sounded like he almost reconciled to losing his case.

Mr. Venkat closed his file, sure that he had convinced the bench and won the case.

"Okay, we will proceed to dictate the order," said Justice Rao, and looked at his colleague sitting to his left.

Justice Murthy leaned towards Justice Rao and whispered something to him. Both the Judges of the division bench began to discuss in hushed voices. After a few minutes they seemed to come to a conclusion because both were nodding as if to say 'okay'.

They turned their heads toward their audience.

The stenographer got up to take dictation.

"Alright counselors, the case will be listed again next week for further hearing," said Justice Rama Rao.

The stenographer sat down in her chair.

"But your lordship…," said Mr. Venkat sounding unhappy and perplexed that the matter was being adjourned.

Justice Rama Rao said, "Mr. Venkat, my colleague Justice Murthy says there is probably a more recent Supreme Court decision, passed only a few days ago, which overrules the case law cited by you. This latest decision is not yet reported but you know that we need to see it before we can make any decision. We are obliged to ensure there is no miscarriage of justice. Also, we would like the young advocate here, to have another chance at researching and citing it."

Turning toward the junior advocate the Judge said, "Please do some research about the latest case law and we will hear it next week."

"Much obliged your lordship," said the junior advocate, picking up his file. He turned around and exited the court hall feeling happy at the unexpected turn of events.

Mr. Venkat exited as well not looking too happy.

Anwitha overheard two advocates sitting in the row behind her say to each other, " I have a feeling Mr. Venkat knew of the latest Supreme Court ruling that was adverse to his client."

"Yes, I do too. There's no way senior advocate Venkat could not have known…he is always on top of these things."

As the next case was called, Anwitha got up to go out of the court hall to get some fresh air. She bowed to the Bench before she exited the door.

She walked to the edge of the corridor outside court hall no.3 and placed her hands on the railing. She stared at the sprawling Cubbon Park beyond the rear parking lot below. She used to visit that park as a child with her parents and many times with her friends during school picnics. During those days, the High Court building was just another of several red buildings in the park to her.

She turned around to face the court hall. Leaning back on the railings she looked at the high ceiling of the building.

"So...Mr. Venkat was taking advantage of the new lawyer unfamiliar with his area of practice? If Justice Murthy hadn't been alert and aware of the latest law then that case would have been decided unfairly. And if no appeal had been filed either due to lack of money or ignorance of the latest Supreme Court decision, it would have resulted in a permanent serious error. Thank goodness for these learned and hardworking Judges...," she thought.

Couple of advocates passed by her. They said "hello".

She waved them "hi".

She looked at her watch. Since it was going to be a while before her case would be called, she decided to go have some coffee. As she walked along the corridor, she peeked into one of the court halls on the way. She saw Sharan in court hall 6. She went inside the court and sat down in the chair next to him.

He looked at her and said, "Hi!" in a hushed tone.

"Hi!"

They sat quietly and observed the proceedings. Court hall 6 was presided over by a single Judge, Justice Raghu.

"My lord, this case has been adjourned two times already. We will need to argue it today," Mr. Pratap, a senior advocate, was submitting.

For the opposing side was a recently enrolled lawyer, barely twenty two years old. Anwitha knew her to be from her own alma mater, and a couple of years junior to her in law college and guessed that she had just graduated. The baby lawyer looked terrified and was looking over her shoulders to see if her senior was there yet.

The Judge asked her, "Are you ready ma'm?"

She just managed to say, "Um…my, my senior is held up in court hall one. Um, please…plead for a pass over my lord. He can be here in the afternoon," by the sound of it, it seemed like it was her first ever submission in court.

Mr. Pratap said vehemently, "I need to be at the Tax Tribunal in the afternoon. We need to hear this now my lord."

Mr. Pratap said glaring at the new lawyer, "She is here," and looking up at the Judge he said, "She can argue the case?!"

Mr. Pratap knew the new lawyer wasn't prepared to argue the case. Everyone in the court hall could guess she wasn't prepared to argue the case.

"Hmm," Justice Raghu leaned back in his chair.

Without turning his head, Sharan leaned slightly toward Anwitha and whispered, "Poor newbie! Trapped here with senior advocate Pratap."

"Yeah poor thing. I guess she was only asked to hold the fort until her senior is done with his case in a different court and Mr. Pratap wants to take advantage of the situation," Anwitha said, looking down.

"The Judge is able to see that," Sharan said, observing the Judge was showing no hurry and was contemplating about how to deal with Mr. Pratap.

Mr. Pratap had the reputation of being one of the very shrewd lawyers in the city who adopted all sorts of tricks to win a case.

Anwitha said, "Hmm. That's the second time this kind of thing is happening in the High Court today,"

"What?"

"A senior lawyer taking advantage of an inexperienced lawyer."

"Hmm, it happens quite often."

Justice Raghu asked the new lawyer, "Counselor, will you argue the case if the case is called after half hour?"

She said, "Um, your lordship…, I have been instructed to seek a pass over. My senior has stated to me that this case is very complicated for me to argue…I may jeopardize the client's case your honor,"

Anwitha and Sharan were watching intently.

Justice Raghu said, "Don't worry about that," and gave the case file to the clerk and said, "Call the case after thirty minutes."

Senior advocate Pratap bowed and exited the court hall.

Noticing she stood frozen and confused, the Judge said to the newbie, "Haven't you had surprise tests at school? Think of this as something like that. You are bound to encounter such situations quite often in this profession…"

Everyone in the court hall smiled.

The Judge said, "Go through the facts of the case in thirty minutes. Do not worry about the law. Be ready with the facts and we will hear the case."

"Yes, your lordship," the new lawyer bowed, turned around and sat down in the front row. She opened her file and began to read.

Next case was called.

7. Narrow Escape

Anwitha asked Sharan, "Do you want to get some coffee?"

"Sure."

They rose from their seats and quietly exited and walked toward the canteen facing the Vidhana Soudha building.

About half hour later they walked back to their respective court halls feeling refreshed after having a by-two coffee and some freshly fried bajjis at the canteen. As Anwitha bowed and entered court hall 3, she noticed there were only two more cases left to be called before hers and advocates for only one of the cases were present in the court hall. That meant practically only one case before hers.

She went in and sat.

The next case was called. The advocates for the parties went forward with their files. The Judges asked, "Are you ready counselors?"

"Yes your lordships, and it probably would take up the rest of the day."

The Judges addressed everybody in the court hall and said, "You all may leave if you like. We will not be able to take up other matters today."

Many including Anwitha left the court hall. As she exited, Anwitha thought, *"Let me see how the baby lawyer is doing in court hall 6."* She walked over to Justice Raghu's court and sat next to Sharan.

The case was called again.

The new lawyer went forward to submit her case. She looked very nervous but knew the Judge's instructions and orders had to be followed.

"Appear for the petitioner your honor," she said literally shaking.

Mr. Pratap went over to the front desk and opened his file. "Appear for the respondent your lordship."

"Yes counselor, tell me the facts of the case," said Justice Raghu, looking at the new lawyer.

She began to read from her file. "My lord, petitioner is…"

Justice Raghu interrupted and said, "What page number are you reading…?"

She looked up at him, and said, "Page three your lordship."

The Judge opened page three of his file. He said, "Alright, you may continue,"

She continued reading. Mr. Pratap flipped the pages in his file to the same page.

The Judge figured out the case within five minutes of browsing through the file but sat back in his chair and allowed the new lawyer to continue for a while to encourage her.

After about fifteen minutes and a couple of questions to the new lawyer, Justice Raghu turned to Mr. Pratap, and asked, "So what do you say?"

Mr. Pratap said, "Petitioner's request cannot be granted because…"

The new lawyer became very nervous listening to her opponent's arguments. She hardly understood what he was saying and didn't know how she should respond. But the Judge who was knowledgeable in the law on the subject matter put tough questions to Mr. Pratap.

After about twenty minutes the Judge said, "So…the facts are established and undisputed. The law is in favor of the client of this young counsel."

Anwitha smiled as the Judge dictated the order incorporating the submissions made by both lawyers and disposed off the matter.

Handing the file to the bench clerk, Justice Raghu smiled at the new lawyer and said, "Good job counselor! See, there is no need to be nervous. Just come prepared with the facts and we will help with the law."

The new lawyer bowed and turned to leave. She looked at Anwitha and Sharan and smiled at them. They smiled back, happy for their friend.

She walked out of the court hall beaming with pride.

Sharan said, leaning toward Anwitha, "The Judge saved the newbie!"

"Yeah, second time today," said Anwitha.

Just then, Sharan's colleague from his firm walked in.

He sat next to Sharan and said to him, "Your presence is needed in the Magistrate's court. I can wait here."

Sharan gave him the file he was holding, and went out. Anwitha followed him and they both started walking towards the rear parking lot.

Sharan asked, "So, did you hear from anyone?"

Anwitha realized he was asking about her LLM program and said, "I heard from WBU. They are offering me full tuition scholarship."

"Hey congrats! When are you leaving?"

"I need to be there by August end."

"Ok let me know once you book your plane tickets. I can have someone pick you up from the airport when you arrive in California."

"Thanks so much Sharan!"

"You are welcome! Okay, catch you later."

"Okay. bye,"

***

"Bring the double murder case file. It is on my desk," Peter Williams told the law clerk over the phone.

"Okay, will bring it right now?"

"Yes. Right now," he disconnected the call.

Peter was in his early forties, six feet three inches tall, well built, had a handsome face with blue eyes, sharp nose and light brown hair.

Lying down on his bed he looked at the poster hung on the wall opposite to him in his bedroom. It had a chart of goals he had set out to achieve in his life. Ivy league law school, Prosecutor, District Attorney, Mayor or Attorney General, Governor, President. There were also certain parallel goals not listed on the chart. Have lots of girlfriends during college, get married to a good looking rich lawyer, or to a good looking daughter of a rich lawyer or politician, buy a home in a posh neighborhood, have three kids by around age thirty five, have a vacation home in at least two locations, may be in Florida or San Diego and Tahoe, for summer and winter.

He had achieved everything he had set out so far. He earned his law degree from an Ivy league law school, was the DA, married to a corporate lawyer who's late father had served as a governor of a state. They had three kids. They lived in a nice home in the posh Palo Alto area. Currently his kids had gone with their mother to attend a relative's wedding in a different city. He had given the excuse of work and given it a miss. It was a perfect opportunity for him to have his intern over at his home who was willing to cooperate…due to her own ambition and competition with other colleagues. They had spent the evening negotiating her career advancement.

He heard the faucet in the bathroom turn off. Couple minutes later, the twenty two year old slim and tall intern exited, with her long dark hair tied in a pony tail.

She picked up her bag.

"I'll let myself out," she said, walking out of the room.

"Okay,"

He switched the TV on and began to browse through the channels. There was an interview of him on one of the talk shows about a case he had won recently which had received wide media attention in the region. He watched his interview intently, satisfied with how the path to the next step in his career was being paved.

He heard some footsteps approach and the intern walked back into the room. He looked up at her and noticed she had a bulky file in her hand.

"The law clerk was downstairs. He had brought this to give you?" she said.

"Oh yes. Thanks. I forgot to bring it before leaving today. The case is tomorrow for opening statement."

She handed him the file and left.

He opened the file and found the draft opening statement. It was prepared by a new young attorney who had joined his office recently.

"Hmm, pretty impressive for someone from a different state and so young. She didn't need any further instructions from me," he thought reading the notes.

He switched the TV off, picked up his laptop and began composing an email to the new young attorney.

"She is smart and pretty," he paused typing and made a couple of edits. *"So young, far from home...hardworking, even though it is an unpaid internship,"* leaning back, he reviewed the email.

"Hello there,

Would like you to work on a research project concerning an important case. You will need to stay a bit longer than usual so I can brief you on the case tomorrow. Meet me at my office at 6 p.m. tomorrow(Friday).

-Peter."

He clicked the send button.

"Everyone usually leaves around 5 p.m. on Fridays," he smiled and got up to shower.

Much accomplished at a young age, Peter wrote scholarly articles, gave talks and lectures on complex topics related to criminal and constitutional laws around the country. He was charming and friendly but had a big ego and was ruthless toward anyone who seemed to be a challenge or competition to him. He was very shrewd, ambitious and mostly adopted fair means to accomplish them but mercilessly put down any impediment in his path. He was so proud of his own achievements and so set on his ambitious goals that he had lost his humility. Because of this, he was unable to take in the right spirit if any occasional oversight, irregularity or imperfections in his work was pointed out.

Fifteen minutes later he exited the shower and got dressed. He picked up his laptop and the file the law clerk had brought home and went to the kitchen. He opened the fridge and looked inside. Nothing in it interested him. He checked a couple of cabinets and then ordered for a pizza.

He went over to the kitchen island and sat on the bar stool, opened his laptop and checked his emails to see if the new young attorney had replied. There was nothing. He closed the laptop and let out a sigh.

***

Half hour later the pizza was delivered. He began eating it and went through the case file. It was a high profile case and the whole of California was talking about it.

He made some notes on the file, closed it and checked his emails again. There was nothing from the new attorney.

It was 10 p.m. He went to the bedroom and brushed his teeth. Then lying down in his bed, switched the TV on. The news channels were talking about the case he was going to handle the next day.

After about twenty minutes he checked the emails again. Nothing from the new attorney.

He switched the TV off and slept.

***

Next morning the alarm buzzed at 6 a.m. Peter snoozed it, picked up his laptop and clicked on his email icon.

"If she hasn't replied yet, need to give her a stern warning to check her emails regularly and promptly reply...wait till I see her today!" he thought, logging in.

There it was, the reply from the new attorney to his email.

"Mr. Peter Williams,

Thank you for trusting me with this responsibility. Unfortunately I cannot accept it because I need to resign from this internship with effect from today. Appreciate your support and the valuable experience I gained working with you.

Sincerely apologize for resigning with short notice.

Thanks,

-Mia Williams."

He slammed the laptop and got out of his bed.

"I certainly don't believe that!"

***

The interviewer told Mia, "We would need a specialist in a few months…we can sponsor your higher studies for specialization if you agree to work for us for a minimum of…"

"Sure, I'm okay with that," Mia said.

"Okay. Another thing. The firm would encourage all of our attorneys to participate in the pro bono program..."

"I would like to as well."

"Great! You are hired!"

8. Unseen Justice

"Lawyers are paid not just for researching and arguing a case, but also for waiting in court and following it up. Actually, researching and arguing is the easy part...," Anwitha remembered what her senior always said.

"That is so true," she thought, standing in the corridor outside of court hall 6. She was a bit tired of sitting inside the court hall for too long. A lengthy argument by a senior counsel was currently being heard and there were four more cases listed before hers and most of the advocates in those matters were present and apparently ready to argue. There was a very slim chance of her case reaching in less than two hours, but one never knew what might happen, especially in the court of Justice Raghu. So she had to wait anyways.

She leaned against the railing. Her cell phone buzzed.

A text message said, "Can you ask for a pass over for me in CH 6, if you are there? Mine is hearing matter no. 3, before yours. I'm stuck in traffic!" It was from Sharan.

"Sure, but it's unlikely to reach any time soon. Relax!" she replied.

Fifteen minutes later she saw him walk down the corridor towards her.

"Hey!" he smiled.

She smiled back and said, "Hi, it is still the first hearing matter."

"Oh ok."

"That's a nice salwar kameez you are wearing. Hema loves this kind of embroidery," he said.

"Thank you! It's called kasuti embroidery,"

"Ok,"

"What else? How are you?"

"Great! I will be flying to Delhi tomorrow, there is a matter before the Supreme Court I need to assist my senior counsel with," said Sharan leaning on the railing beside her.

"Wow! How exciting!" she said, " Hey that reminds me…earlier this year, I guess in March, the Supreme Court has admitted an appeal by the accused in Jessica Lall murder case right? Why do you think the Supreme

Court did that? I feel the appeal should not have been admitted in the first place."

"Well, I think it was necessary," said Sharan.

"Why?"

"Simply because, justice must not only be done but manifestly and undoubtedly be seen to be done."

Anwitha smiled at that and nodded. "Yes, justice must be seen to be done," she said.

"Yes! See, it was no ordinary case. The son of a former member of Parliament shoots and kills a celebrity waitress. This happened at a party attended by who's who of the country. So the crime was witnessed by several famous and powerful people, including some media personnel. The entire nation knew about what happened, who the murderer was…almost immediately after the murder. A trial was only a formality to be fulfilled before sentencing the accused, so that…"

"Justice is also seen to be done!" Anwitha finished it for him and laughed.

"Right!" Sharan laughed as well and continued, "But then what happened? Although there were hundreds of credible witnesses, almost all of them turned hostile during trial or refused to testify. So, the Trial Court acquitted the accused for lack of evidence,"

He paused for a moment and continued, "Or because the court thought there was lack of legally acceptable evidence…"

He looked down at Anwitha. She was listening intently.

He said, "To add insult to injury, around this time, the father of the accused had become the minister in Haryana state government…the citizens felt betrayed by the system and there was a huge public outcry. See, one didn't need in depth knowledge of the law to see that the acquittal was wrong in this case, regardless of the technical reasons the trial Judge had given,"

Anwitha nodded, remembering the candle light vigils and protest marches throughout the country in 2006, following the acquittal. The news media covered the case in a way that even a person who hardly followed any current events could not miss it.

Sharan continued, "In view of the angry reaction of the public, the first appellate court, the High Court of Delhi, took suo motu action, and called for the records of the case from the prosecution without waiting for the prosecution to file the appeal…which is very, very rare."

Anwitha said, "True."

"The High Court of Delhi re-heard the case and convicted the accused. Now, in view of contradictory verdicts by the High Court and the Trial Court, it is better that finality is reached by a ruling of the Supreme Court. The accused should be given, and it should be seen that he is given a reasonable opportunity to defend himself and is not convicted through media trial."

"Yes, I see what you mean. it is good if the Supreme Court settles the matter in a case followed by the whole country,"

"Yep, oh!" he looked into court hall 6. "That hearing is over! Let's go inside."

"There's still some time for mine to reach. I'll have some coffee and come back."

"We have one more, later in the list, contesting each other. Are you ready?"

"Of course. Our clients are here, waiting."

"Yeah…puzzled and worried too," Sharan glanced at the men pacing up and down the adjacent terrace. "They are staring at us."

"Hmm. It's hard for them to understand how opposing lawyers can be friends."

"Yeah. They'll know they worried for nothing when they see us argue...ok, go have your coffee," he went inside the court hall.

***

The canteenwallah smiled at Anwitha. "Coffee madam?"

"Houdu," she smiled.

It began to rain.

Somebody said, "Typical Bangalore weather! Can never tell when it will rain,"

"Or for how long!"

Everyone moved away from the railing and huddled in the middle of the terrace.

"Tagolli madam," the canteen guy handed her a little steel cup of coffee. She took a sip and stared at the Vidhana Soudha across the street.

"Need to go to Chennai next week for my visa interview...," she took another sip.

Suddenly it was sunny and bright, although still raining.

"Oh god! I still haven't told my parents about getting accepted to US LLM program!"

9. New World

Anwitha told her mother during the weekend about her LLM program and that she would be leaving in about three weeks' time to America. Just as she expected, all hell broke loose when the news reached her father. She tried hard to convince him it was going to be alright but he was still upset.

"So no plans of marrying and settling down?" he had yelled.

"Who knows, she might find someone in the Bay Area. The place is full of Indian techies," her mother had tried to calm her father down.

Anwitha's mother Sumitra was fifty six and looked much younger. She was always busy, doing either housework or tutoring the neighborhood kids. Anwitha's father Nagraj Bhat worked as a librarian. He worried that he would retire soon as he was turning sixty five that year and wished to see his only child married by then.

"Okay do whatever you like. You don't seem to care about what I think," he had said to Anwitha.

"No need to worry, I will get married one day. Just not right now. I'm sure it would all work out fine, " she had said.

Sometimes Anwitha had difficulty knowing whether her parents considered her their responsibility or liability.

"I'll transfer some money to your account. How much do you think you will need?" he had asked, yielding to her finally.

"I have savings. Besides I'm getting full scholarship," she'd told him.

"Never mind. Having some reserve fund is good. Especially, when you are living in a foreign country," her dad had insisted.

***

"Hey what's up?" said Sharan picking up Anwitha's call.

"Hi!! Calling from Chennai! My visa is granted!"

"Oh great! Congrats!"

"Thanks!"

"What did your parents say?"

"Well, they are not too comfortable. But have said okay,"

"Hmmm, when are you leaving?"

"By the end of August."

"Will let Hema's uncle in California know. He can help you out with accommodation and everything."

"Okay, thank you!"

"You are welcome! We are at the Kempe Gowda tower right now after visiting the flower show at Lal Bagh. Hema is so amazed at the view of Bangalore from up here. The city looks so beautiful!"

"Yeah, it's been ages since I went there last."

"Me too, re-living my childhood days."

"Alright enjoy! Bye,"

"Bye, you'll be in Bangalore when?"

"Tomorrow. My train just arrived."

"Ok."

***

Anwitha informed her colleagues in the law firm about her decision to take a sabbatical to do her LLM in the United States of America. While everyone was happy for her, they were sad they would miss her as well.

"So when are you leaving?" Mr. Srinivas asked.

"In two weeks."

"Okay, good luck! Hope you make us all proud!"

"Thanks!" she said.

"Well, I hope I can survive first," she thought to herself.

While she was acting really brave outwardly, she was really fearful of what life would be like in a foreign country where she did not know anyone. She had actually grown more fearful of the people who seemed to make her feel insecure because she was not married yet. While she was afraid to marry a wrong guy under pressure, she was afraid of remaining unmarried too, or running out of options and of good suitors, and eventually compromising because she had grown too old. She just needed to get away to clear her mind. She thought this LLM opportunity would give her the necessary break to hone her career credentials and to think things through calmly before she could choose her life partner.

***

Later that day she finished all the work in the cases assigned to her and went to have coffee in the canteen. As she sipped her hot coffee she looked at the Vidhana Soudha, the beautiful white building in front of her. Then she looked at the red High Court building that stretched out on either side of the terrace she was standing on.

She thought to herself, *"I'll be missing all this when I leave next month. My beautiful city Bengaluru, these court halls, my family, friends, speaking in Kannada, Hindi, Telugu, Tamil, Malayalam, Hinglish, Kinglish...shopping on MG Road, Commercial Street, eating yummy street food, chaat..."*

***

Anwitha boarded the Singapore Airlines on 20th August 2007 and sat in her seat next to the window. This was her first international flight. She messaged her parents and switched her phone off.

She would first fly to Singapore, then to Hong Kong and then finally finish the last leg of fourteen hours to San Francisco. Total travel time including layovers would be thirty six hours. She had no problem with that.

"I'll catch up on some movies," she thought.

"During the layover at Singapore I should check out that famous butterfly garden in Changi airport..."

***

At its scheduled time, the plane slowly took off, and as Anwitha looked down through the window at the spectacular night view of the vast city of Bengaluru, a million memories flashed through her mind.

"Bye now, Bangalore,"

She kept looking out until she was able to catch the last glimpse of her city, before the plane flew far into the darkness towards its destination.

***

Two flights and thirty five hours later-
"The local time now is 11 a.m., passengers are requested to wear their seat belts," said the announcement.

Anwitha woke up from her sleep.

The plane had begun to slowly descend to land in the airport at San Francisco. She saw on the monitor the roughly edged '8' kind of shape the sea had carved into the land mass that is called the San Francisco Bay Area. She looked out the window and saw part of the region near the SF airport. The place looked urban with many buildings, busy streets and plenty of natural beauty with green hills, little islands, lagoons and backwaters. She spotted a really long bridge over a part of the bay.

A kid in the front row yelled, "Look! There's the San Mateo bridge, it's twelve miles long!"

His mom said, "Yeah, it's one of the four major bridges in Bay Area."

***

"Over 100,000 innocents are in U.S. prisons for crimes they didn't commit…"

She tied her soft brown hair in a bun and continued to review the research findings for the pro bono matter assigned to her.

"Many non profit organizations are working to eliminate the causes of wrongful convictions. Some of them are…"

***

Anwitha exited the airport and looked around. An Indian gentleman aged around fifty came up to her and said, "Gopalan. Sharan's uncle in law. You are Anwitha?"

"Yes,"

He extended his hand. She shook it.

"Welcome to America!! I'm here to receive you and take you to your accommodation." he said.

"Thanks so much!"

"No problem! Let's go?"

"Yes,"

"This way,"

She followed him with her luggage cart to the parking lot. "Would you prefer to be addressed by your name or ...," she asked.

"Oh, you can call me uncle! I still address desis elder to me as uncle or aunty or something similar whether related or not,"

"Okay, uncle!"

"How was the flight?"

"Very long and tiring...had a nice break at Changi airport and Hong Kong though."

"Ha ha okay...did you have any problem at the customs or immigration?"

"No, not at all."

"They always check my bags for Jeera!"

"Ha ha!"

As they reached the car, she said, "I was going to call you, great you were able to recognize me. You had emailed me a picture of yours but I guess you look a bit different in the picture?"

"Ha ha, yes, I could recognize you from the picture and the initials on your luggage, A.N.B.? Thought it might be you."

"Oh okay," she smiled.

They loaded her bags in the trunk and sat in the car. She sat in the right front seat, which would be the driver's seat in India. When Gopal uncle wore his seat belt she remembered it was mandatory in this country. She quickly wore her seat belt as well. Gopal uncle carefully pulled out of the parking spot and drove slowly out of the airport. Although she knew about it before, Anwitha felt it really weird that he was driving on the right side of the street which would be the wrong side in India. Few minutes later, their car entered into a free way. As they drove she saw how smooth the traffic was moving. There were no people to be seen anywhere, mostly cars. No scooter, not many motorbikes. Few delivery trucks. What struck her the most was that there was hardly any noise, despite the busy traffic. No honking, no one applying sudden breaks or coming to a screeching halt.

Taking in the scenery around her from inside the car, she thought, *"So this is the land Columbus came to while trying to find a sea route to India...,"* wondering what the world would have been like, had he not got lost.

"Hmm, it must be midnight in India now. The time difference is approximately twelve hours, this time of the year."

"Here, do you need to let your parents know you have arrived safely? You can use my cell phone," Gopal uncle took the phone out of his pocket.

"Yes, thanks."

Anwitha took the phone and sent a text message to her mother's cell phone.

"Arrived safely. Will call."

"Okay," came the reply just seconds later.

"Amma was still awake and waiting for my message." she gave the phone back to Gopal uncle.

***

They reached the apartment building in San Carlos city in less than half hour. At the manager's office, they signed the lease papers and got the key to her apartment.

It was a cute little apartment with an open kitchen and living room area, a short hallway leading to the bedroom and a bathroom to the right. There was a balcony accessible from the living room and the bedroom which overlooked the street outside.

"It's pretty large," thought Anwitha.

Once all her bags were in, Gopal uncle asked, "Do you like the apartment?"

"Yes!!"

"Great! You should have the internet and landline phone by this evening. I'll leave now to work, I have ordered your food from a nearby restaurant. In about ten minutes your lunch will be delivered," he said.

"Oh! You shouldn't have, uncle!"

"No problem. Okay let me know if you need anything. Please do not hesitate."

"Can you help me get a cell phone?"

"Yes, sure."

"Thanks so much!"

"You are welcome. Bye now,"

***

She closed the apartment door and went over to the balcony. Across the street was a row of beautiful two storey homes set against green hills.

"Such a nice view!" she went inside, showered and wore her pajamas and took out all the perishable snacks her mother had packed in her suitcase and put them in the fridge.

The doorbell rang. There was a man with the delivery from the nearby restaurant.

She took the bag. *"Hmm. desi food!"*

"How much is it?"

"It has been paid for madam, enjoy," the man left.

She ate the curd rice and put the lemon rice in the fridge for dinner. She felt sleepy.

But Sharan had warned her to wait until dark to sleep as it would otherwise be more difficult to overcome the jet lag.

She removed an idol of Ganesha from her suitcase, placed it on a little 'stand' she made out of the books she'd got, and meditated.

At four p.m. a local cable guy arrived to set up the internet and phone connections. Anwitha called her mother and talked for an hour. Well actually, listened to all the admonitions and cautions.

"Let me go for a walk and explore the place. Need some groceries too and something to sleep on."

***

"Could you do the closing arguments in Rosa Lopez vs. AZ cars?"

Mia looked up at the senior associate standing across her desk.

"The personal injury case?"

"Yes, I cannot. Something came up. Will be out of town that day."

"Oh god. I'm nervous!"

"You've drafted the closing arguments, it's pretty good. You know the case well."

"Sure!" said Mia.

***

Anwitha spread the sleeping bag on the carpeted floor and checked her emails. She dozed off at 7 p.m. with many random thoughts running through her mind.

"I should figure out the public transport system here…Friday is the orientation in law school…need some furniture…"

Eventually thoughts coalesced into dreams…

She was at her LLM class listening to a lecture. Suddenly her cell phone rang. It was from home. "There's a good marriage proposal. The boy's family will be visiting us tonight…you come home right now!!"

10. Confluence

"I feel so alien and alone...hope I make some good friends here," Anwitha walked into the campus of West Bay University School of Law in San Francisco. It had only been three days since she landed in California and was still jet lagged.

She was about half hour early for the new students' orientation session. She spent some time exploring the campus. It had some really nice landscape and garden. It was summer time in California and the plants were all in full bloom. There were daisies, dahlias, oregano, lavender and little rose bushes. She noticed several butterflies fluttering over some of the flowers, especially the oregano.

She was fascinated with butterflies ever since she was a little girl and never quite got over it. Once in her school she had done a project on metamorphosis and transformation of butterflies and won a prize for it. She had closely observed how from an egg a worm is born, which transforms into a cocoon, eventually emerging as a beautiful butterfly having absolutely no resemblance to its previous forms in the way it moved, fed, appeared or functioned. But it is the same life. The teacher who had helped her in the project would explain, *"We have to look at nature and learn. The butterfly couldn't happen prior to the happening of the worm or the egg. To develop its wings it had to be all its prior forms for a while. At the right time, it would have to cast off the characteristics of its previous forms to develop new and more advantageous ones...there is no other way. If it had remained inside the egg, it wouldn't develop into a worm and if it remained a worm it wouldn't become a butterfly!"*

Just then she heard some squealing at a distance. She turned her head and saw some students cruising into the campus on their skateboards racing with each other. A smile crossed her lips.

"So nice to be a college student again!" she checked the time and began to walk to the class room where the orientation was to be held. Along the way she noticed several

squirrels running up the trees and playing on the lawn.

"The entire atmosphere is so cheerful!" she reached the class room and opened the door.

There were three students inside. Two of them were on the left side, huddled together. She walked in and climbed up to the third row on the right and sat down on the bench at the far right side. In front of her, in the first row, a girl with brown hair sat engrossed in something she was reading. She was wearing a formal pant suit. Anwitha got up, went to the first row and sat on the far left side of the bench. The girl turned and looked at Anwitha.

"Hi," she said. She had a pretty smile.
"Hi"
"I'm Anwitha."
"I'm Mia."
"Where are you from?" Mia asked.
"India."
"Oh, India!" she smiled and said, "I was in India for a few months, as a JD student. It was part of the student exchange program."
"Oh really?!"
"Yes. I was there for about five months!"
"Oh! Where?! Which part of India?"

Anwitha certainly didn't expect to meet a non Indian who had been to India on her first day at law school.

"The place was Bangalore, Khaarnatakha, in southern part of India. Sorry for my pronunciation…I was there for several months but still can't pronounce some of the words correctly,"

"It's okay, I have trouble pronouncing foreign names too."

"You are so kind," Mia smiled, picked up her bag and came closer to Anwitha and sat.

"I am from that state, Karnataka," Anwitha said.

"It's awesome. The place is soo beautiful! The sea, the beaches, the western ghats, the food…and those amazing temples in Hampi, Beloor and Halebid. Oh my god!"

"Ha ha, thanks!"

"Also, Goa was so close too! I could visit Goa like at least three times while I was there!"

"Yeah! The State of Karnataka borders with Goa,"

"Hmm,"

Mia said, "I wish I could visit many other places in India you know, there is just so much to see there…but, I was busy with my projects and assignments…and then I had to return for my next semester here."

"Well, you can always visit again!"

"Oh yes! I certainly would love to!"

"So how do you like California so far?" Mia asked.

"Well, I haven't seen much of it. It's been only three days since I landed here. I like it so far. Just settling down in my apartment. I like San Carlos, where I'm currently living,"

"Okay," Mia said nodding her head. She said, "I'm new here as well…I'm from Florida originally. Did my JD there, and practiced for a couple of years…recently passed the California Bar exam," she smiled.

Anwitha smiled back and said, "Oh! Wow!!"

"Thanks!"

"Why are you doing the Masters then?"

"I needed to specialize, and my employer is paying for it."

"Okay,"

By this time, more students had arrived in the class room and it was full.

"Good morning everyone!"

The Assistant Dean, LLM Director, Law Student Services representative and the Librarian walked in.

"Welcome to West Bay University school of Law!" the LLM Director introduced the Assistant Dean, the librarian and a couple of former LLM students. Each of them gave a small speech about the program, the university and a general outline about the life of a student of the Master of Laws program.

After the speeches were over, the students were asked to introduce themselves.

"Hello, I'm Heidy, I did my JD in Texas."

"Hi I'm Heejin from South Korea."

"Hi I'm Mia from Florida."

"I'm Anwitha from India."

"I'm from Germany,"

"I'm from Taiwan…"

***

As they were going out of the class, Mia asked, "So, what are you doing in the afternoon?"

"I don't know. May be just go home, eat lunch and do the laundry I guess?"Anwitha laughed.

Mia laughed and asked, "I have some work later in San Mateo Superior Court. Do you want to come?"

"Sure!"

"We can grab some lunch on the way."

"Sounds good!"

They walked to the parking lot where Mia had parked her car. As they walked, Anwitha noticed how Mia had a very attractive personality.

"I got this only last week!"said Mia as she opened the door to the driver's seat of her small car.

Anwitha said smiling, "It's cute! I like small cars too, so much easier to drive,"

"I know right?!"

"Yeah…the car I drove in India was also small like this. I mostly see huge SUVs and big cars here. It is refreshing to see something small and cute!"

"Ha ha. Thanks."

They both sat in the car.

"Are you a vegetarian?"asked Mia as she began to pull out of the parking lot.

"Yes," Anwitha smiled.

"Well, we can have lunch in Downtown Redwood City. There are a lot of Mexican restaurants there, which have vegetarian choices."

"Sure."

"Thanks," Anwitha added.

In the last three days' of her stay in the United States she had learned that people here said thanks a lot more often, almost for every little thing. In many of similar situations, if she said thanks to people in India, they would certainly take offense.

"You are Welcome!!" said Mia.

Looking at the clock in her car Mia said, "I should be in court for a closing argument in the afternoon. Although I've temporarily quit doing court work since I enrolled for my LLM, I was asked to handle this case because I've researched and drafted the closing argument. The trial is almost over and the closing argument is the only stage left…I do hope the jury will decide in my client's favor…"

Anwitha turned and looked at Mia.

"By jury…do you mean a panel of Judges?!" she asked.

Mia stopped when the traffic light turned red. "No…!!?" she said.

She turned and looked at Anwitha, surprised.

She thought for a moment and said, "It consists of…a panel…of ordinary citizens…"

"Hmm."

Anwitha didn't understand. But she asked nothing more.

"Did I ask a stupid question? Was I supposed to know it?"

She remembered Sharan saying to her once, *"You hardly know anything outside your immediate work!"*

"But when I do know something, I make sure I know everything about it!" she had replied.

"When I get back home I'll do some research on the 'Jury'...," she thought.

The lights turned green and Mia stepped on the accelerator.

"What do you plan to do after LLM?" asked Mia.

"I don't know, I would like to practice here for a little while, if circumstances permit."

Anwitha looked at the ring on Mia's hand. *"She's married? She's quite young. Probably same age as me,"*

"Do you have a boyfriend?" Mia asked.

Anwitha said, "No."

"Do you?" Anwitha didn't want to ask if she was married, as she was not sure if the ring was indeed a wedding ring.

"I have a husband!!" Mia laughed. "We are leaving for a short honeymoon next weekend."

"Oh! Congrats! You were married recently…?"

"Yeah, everything happened in short notice."

"Great! Where are you going?"

"Aruba!"

"Wow! Hope you have a wonderful honeymoon!"

"Thank you!"

Mia parked the car and got out. Anwitha got out and looked around the downtown area in Redwood City. Ahead of the street was an arch saying 'Theatre District'.

Mia put some coins in the parking meter. "This way Anwitha," Mia said, leading the way.

Anwitha followed.

"Did I say your name right?"

"Yes! Thank you Mia."

They walked into a self service Mexican restaurant.

"You could try veggie burritos. It is a tortilla wrap with rice, beans, vegetables, cheese and sauces," Mia suggested.

Mia ordered one for herself also.

They sat at a table with their burritos and tortilla chips. "What time is your case going to be heard?" Anwitha asked.

"Soon after the lunch break. We have enough time. No rush," Mia smiled.

Anwitha smiled and asked, "What is the case about?"

"It's a personal injury case," Mia said taking a bite of her burrito. "I'm excited and nervous. It's going to be my first closing argument ever!"

Anwitha smiled nodding her head and said, "I understand. I know that feeling very well. Wish you all the best!"

"Thanks!"

Half hour later they were in the courtroom. Mia had explained how they called it a courtroom in California.

Anwitha sat in the audience section. Mia went beyond the railing which she called 'the bar or the well,' that separated the audience section from the rest of the courtroom. She sat at a desk next to her client. Anwitha noticed that at the very front of the courtroom, on a raised platform was the Judge's bench, flanked by the California State flag and the United States flag. Directly in front of the Judge's bench was a table on which piles of files were kept and the court clerks were arranging them and making some notes in their register. To the left of the Judge's seat was a witness box and to the right, against the wall, was another large box with two rows of upholstered chairs.

"Everything is pretty much like Indian trial courts except for the security men near the entrance door of each courtroom…"

Anwitha sighed.

"…And also for that big box with those empty chairs…there are about twelve of them…"

The Judge walked in and everyone rose.

"What is that box?"

The Judge took his seat and everyone sat down.

11. The Box

The bench clerk called the case and handed the file to the Judge. Mia stood and said, "For the plaintiff."

The opposing attorney said, "For the defendant."

"Plaintiff ready for closing statement?" asked the Judge.

"Yes," Mia said.

"Defendant ready?"

"Yes,"

"Call the jury."

"Yes, your honor." A bailiff went in through a door beside the box of twelve chairs. He returned after a few seconds and stood next to the door. Following him, twelve persons arrived and sat in the twelve empty chairs. They were aged between thirty five and late fifties and belonged to varied ethnicity and gender.

"They look much like those who are sitting in the audience section...," Anwitha

thought, noticing all the people present in the courtroom.

She turned her attention to Mia. Mia took her notes out of the file and glanced through it. She walked over to the box where the twelve people sat. She took a deep breath and confidently began her closing arguments.

"Ladies and gentlemen of the jury, my client here," Mia turned and pointed at her client, a lady in her early thirties, then turned back towards the jury and continued, "had rented a car from the defendant company last year. While she was driving the rented car on the freeway…the car suddenly spun toward her left and moved in the reverse direction…and eventually slid leftward and hit the road divider and came to a halt. We have, through reliable evidence, established that this happened due to defendant's negligence. The defendant gave my client a defective car and it is the direct and proximate cause of the injuries..."

Mia paused and said, "My client suffered injuries to her back, shoulders and right hand…my client also suffered emotional trauma…We have proved that, the actual damages she has incurred is… the defendant is liable to pay damages of…to my client…thank you."

Mia went back to her seat.

The attorney for the defendant which was a car rental company argued at length as to how there was no negligence. After that, Mia briefly replied refuting the defendant's stance.

The Judge announced, "Ladies and gentlemen of the jury, these are your instructions for deliberations," he began to read from a document, "Negligence is defined as…"

Anwitha looked at the jury members. Some were simply listening to the Judge, while others were making notes.

The Judge continued, "…has the plaintiff established by a preponderance of evidence that the defendant has been negligent? Preponderance of evidence means more likely than not…Is the defendant's negligence the proximate and direct cause of plaintiff's injury…?"

"What is going on…?!" Anwitha thought.

"You shall first select a foreperson to be your chair and spokesperson…The jury may now proceed to the jury room for deliberations," the Judge ordered.

The twelve persons were led out through the same door they had used to walk into the courtroom earlier. The Judge took up some miscellaneous matters after the jury exited to the jury room. Forty five minutes later the bailiff went to the Judge and whispered something. There was an announcement by the bench clerk.

"The jury is ready with their decision in Rosa Lopez vs. AZ Cars."

Anwitha sat upright. *"That is Mia's case,"*

The twelve persons returned and sat in the same chairs, as they did earlier.

Anwitha scanned the courtroom once, looked at the Judge and the court employees he was surrounded by. She looked at the attorneys waiting for their cases. She looked at the security personnel near the door. It struck her why she felt the twelve persons looked like the people in the audience section. They had no connection with the law or judiciary in the same manner as others within the bar area of the courtroom. Like the clients and others sitting in the audience section, they understood some things that were happening in court but they didn't understand a lot of things. Basically they didn't look like they belonged.

"The jury consists of ordinary citizens," she remembered what Mia had said earlier.

The Judge asked, "Respected jury members, are you ready with your decision?"

One of the twelve jury members stood and said, "Yes your honor," and gave a folded note to the bailiff.

The bailiff gave it to the bench clerk who passed it to the Judge. The Judge opened it and read it carefully. Then he read it out loud.

"The jury has unanimously decided…the plaintiff is entitled to a total damages of sixty eight thousand dollars, for the injuries she suffered and attorney fees and costs…"

"Oh! Guess Mia has won her first case! Good for her!!" Anwitha smiled.

***

As they walked out of the Courthouse, Anwitha said to Mia, "Congratulations! You were great!"

"Thanks!"

"Do you want me to drop you home?" Mia asked.

"No, that's okay. I'll take the bus."

"Okay, let me drop you to the bus stop."

"Sure, thanks."

It was 6 p.m. when Anwitha got back to her apartment. She made instant noodles, with spicy desi masala and sat with the plate in front of her laptop.

"I need to know more about the jury system."

Anwitha began her research on the internet. She read everything that came up. It was past midnight when she finally closed the laptop after over five hours. She got up, put the plate in the kitchen sink, went to the bathroom, brushed her teeth and got in her bed.

"I'm probably missing something here...I still do not get it," she fell asleep within seconds.

Before long, *she was in the same courtroom where Mia had argued her case earlier that day. The same Judge sat in his chair presiding over the case. Mia and the defendant's attorney were there as well. But...why were they all wearing medical scrubs?!! There was something else...a table that seemed to resemble the operating tables in hospitals. It was placed in the middle of the courtroom and Mia's client was lying on that table. She seemed pregnant...and looked nervous. The twelve people or whom everyone called the 'jury members' were there...they were also wearing the scrubs...*

Mia was saying to them, "To solve this problem you need to make an incision here, with this surgical instrument...," she was holding up some kind of a knife that surgeons would use. She attempted to hand it to the jury...

Just then the opposing counsel said, "No! This would be a better alternative...," he held up some other tool that looked quite convoluted and scary...

The Judge intervened and told the jury, "Ladies and gentlemen of the jury, these are your instructions according to the medical text books...," he began to read the instructions. He concluded by saying, "And based on this you make a decision as to how to operate, where to cut, how much to cut. Remember to keep the baby and the mother safe..."

The twelve 'jury doctors' seemed to be a bit confused. They began to talk among themselves...no one else could hear what they were discussing...the foreperson took the scalpel from Mia and rolled the operation table along with the patient lying on it, into an adjacent jury room. Other jury members followed him. They closed the door and shut everyone out. Anwitha peered through a window into the jury room to see what was happening. The foreperson held up the scalpel and looked down at the patient, Mia's client. He took a deep breath, as if to make up his mind…and cut Mia's client's tummy…the rest of the 'juror doctors' began to press on her tummy…Anwitha quietly went to the door and pushed it to open slightly, to hear them better.

She heard one juror go, "Oh I hope we are doing it right!"

"Let's just try our best," said one of the women jurors.

"Should we be doing this at all? I'm not sure if we are doing it right…"

"We just have to!! It is our civic duty as the citizens of this country…"

"Well we discussed it all already, didn't we?!"

"Yes…and common wisdom is enough to do this!!"

"I think we should just go ahead and pull the baby out now…"

"No no…wait…we need to make a bigger cut!" an older gentleman in the jury said.

"Are you sure?"

"Yes,"

The foreman gave the scalpel to him. He took it and seemed to cut the patient again.

"There, now it looks better...I think we can try now to take the baby out."

"Yes, go ahead."

They all bent over the patient's tummy.

Unable to look at it any further, Anwitha closed the door behind her and went back to the courtroom. She sat down in one of the chairs and closed her eyes.

Suddenly everyone heard the wailing of the baby! Anwitha opened her eyes.

The foreperson came out with the baby in his arms and announced.

"We have delivered!! Your honor, the mother and the baby are both fine."

He held the baby up for everyone to see.

The Judge said, "Thank you ladies and gentlemen for your services..."

Anwitha was still in a state of shock! Everything seemed hazy...then...she saw them...in the corner of the room, standing quietly. They looked familiar...but she couldn't place.

Anwitha walked towards them to get a closer look...the faces became clear. It was the doctor couple from India facing medical malpractice charges! She remembered them from the photographs she'd seen on TV.

The daddy doctor now came to the middle of the courtroom and started addressing the Judge. The Judge now looked different...he had Justice Raghu's face.

With folded hands, the doctor said to Justice Raghu, "What I did is not different from what just happened here under the direction and supervision of this court and per the orders of this court. My lord, I am not guilty of any kind of criminal offense. My son merely did what the jurors did. I did what the learned Judge just did. The case is exactly similar. Only difference is mine is a medical case while the other case is a legal case."

Justice Raghu seemed perplexed.

The doctor continued to appeal, "A jury trial is like a legal operation performed by unqualified persons...since it is permitted and even endorsed by a common law constitution, a medical operation by unqualified persons supervised by doctors should also be allowed...there is no rational basis for differentiating between medical field and legal field...under the circumstances, it amounts to unfair discrimination to hold me criminally liable for actions similar to those of this court…I pray that I be honorably acquitted of all the charges against me…"

Anwitha stared at the Judge with impatience to hear his decision.

Finally Justice Raghu said, "Reserved for judgment," and exited the courtroom!

12. Dicey Justice

"I miss Mia. The class is so much more interesting when she is also there," Anwitha thought as she walked out of her class.

She sat on one of the benches in the garden. *"Let me send today's notes to Mia right away,"* she reached into the bag for her laptop.

Heidy and Heejin, who were eating their lunch at the table nearby, waved at Anwitha. She waved back and began to compose an email to Mia.

"Want to join us?" Heidy asked.

"Sure, but I didn't bring lunch from home today, got up late so had to rush," Anwitha sent the email and put the laptop back in the bag and walked toward them.

"Oh! We can share my sandwiches. I made lots of them." Heejin held her lunch box out. "There's no meat. Want one?"

"Thanks Heejin," Anwitha smiled and took one.

"It's delicious," she said, taking a bite. "I also had to skip breakfast today and I'm too hungry. I need a big meal. Any restaurant you know of that I can try?"

"Yeah, you could try the Thai restaurant in the corner. They will have veggie choices and it will be filling."

"Okay! Thanks,"

"When is Mia coming back?" Heidy asked.

"Next Monday," Anwitha said.

"Okay,"

"Hope she is having fun in Aruba!" Heejin giggled.

"I'm sure she is," Anwitha said finishing the sandwich. "Alright guys, see you later."

"Bye, see ya,"

Anwitha walked to the Thai restaurant and ordered pad thai with yellow curry. As she ate, she worked on some of her class assignments. After lunch, she walked to an ice cream store nearby and ordered a strawberry ice cream.

"Can I see your ID?" the cashier asked when Anwitha gave him her credit card to pay.

Anwitha showed him her id issued by California Department of Motor Vehicles.

As the cashier examined the id card, a smile crossed Anwitha's lips.

"Someone who stole a credit card will not use it in an ice cream store mister," she thought.

Couple seconds later, he handed her the ice cream. Anwitha took it and sat at one of the tables outside the ice cream store, enjoying the view of the bay.

"It is so beautiful!" she stared at the birds flying over the sparkly ocean dotted with sailboats and ships.

After about half hour, she went back to the campus to complete her assignments in the library. When she finished it was 5 p.m.

"It's time to head back home. I have no time today to continue my research on the jury system," Anwitha thought.

"I have so many questions to ask Mia about it," she packed her bag and left.

***

The door bell rang. It was Gopal uncle.

"Here's your cell phone."

"Thanks so much!"

She wrote him a check for the cost.

"Will you have coffee?" she asked him, handing him the check.

"No, don't bother. I got to run."

"Gopal uncle, where can I buy furniture for cheap?"

"Try Ikea or Amazon, or Craigslist. You may even find something for free,"

"Okay."

"Bye now,"

"Bye."

***

"It's Monday today. I'll get to meet Mia!" Anwitha woke up thinking. She was at the class on time. Mia wasn't there yet.

The professor walked in and said, "Good morning class!"

Anwitha opened her laptop. Just then Mia walked in. Anwitha smiled and Mia smiled back and sat beside her. She looked pretty tanned. The professor began his lecture, and they began taking notes.

After an hour the professor said, "Okay! that brings us to the end of this class," and picked up his things to leave. Everyone began to close their laptops and books and began to leave as well.

The next class for Mia and Anwitha was in the same class room, so they remained seated.

Anwitha turned to Mia and said, "Hi! How was your little vacation?"

Mia said, "Awesome!! Here, let me show you the pictures,"

"Wow! So beautiful! I want to go there!" Anwitha said.

"Yeah you should!"

The professor for their next class walked in. "Good morning!"

"Now let's review what we discussed in our last class before we start," the professor said. "The best feature of common law is it can evolve and adapt…"

***

After the class was over, Anwitha and Mia bought sandwiches from the school cafeteria and sat down at a table outside to eat. It was sunny and there were a few squirrels scurrying on the green lawns. Anwitha noticed how they were bigger than the ones in India and had no lines on their backs. But they were just as cute. Staying in Bay Area Anwitha did not miss India that much. There were many expatriates and students from India and many Indian events were organized throughout the year. Indian food and restaurants were available in virtually every part of Bay Area. The weather was sunny and got more tropical in the southern parts of California. San Jose and Santa Clara were pretty warm although it was much chillier in winter than Bangalore.

"So how do you find your LLM program so far?" Mia asked cutting Anwitha's thoughts.

"It's great! Pretty intense but I'm enjoying it so far," said Anwitha.

"Uh huh," Mia took a bite of her sandwich.

"Hey Mia," said Anwitha wiping her hands with a napkin.

"Hmm?"

"I'm trying to understand the American jury system. You know in India, they would have in each village a governing and judicial body called the Panchayat...they still do in many parts of India even today. The members of the Panchayat, called the Panchas would be the ordinary residents of the village. Usually, the wise and respected elders would be chosen by the local community as members of the Panchayat. They routinely performed administrative and adjudicating functions in the village, and settled disputes between individuals within their village and also between neighboring villages. They would not be formally educated or trained in law or administration, but over the years they gained the expertise functioning as the Panchas. Is the jury system something like that?"

"Um, no. Well, the jury system is based on the common wisdom of ordinary people. The early European settlers in America brought it with them when they immigrated to this part of the world. This is how the jury system works. First a pool of randomly selected individuals are summoned. Some of them with acceptable excuses are let go. The remaining persons are screened by the attorneys of all parties to the dispute…for any bias, preconceived notions etc., and then picked or let go. Each party is given a specific number of challenges without cause and unlimited number of strikes for cause…"

"What are the qualifications for the juror?"

"US citizenship, age at least 18, certain level of English proficiency and no prior convictions. But these are technical qualifications," Mia paused for a moment. "But…in practice persons who are highly educated, engineers, PhD holders and lawyers, law students are eliminated."

"Why?"

"Because they are considered too methodical and hard to convince. They make the job of the lawyer difficult. I've seen it happen in personal injury cases. My boss would tell me, ideally a middle aged taxi driver is the best juror for the plaintiff in a personal injury case," Mia paused again and continued, "Also because other jury members will probably look at the individual who is highly qualified or has a law background for guidance and so may get influenced by such better qualified co-juror. In that case it will not be a decision by the panel of jurors...but a decision by that particular individual's alone seconded by others."

"Hmm, but if that is so, in the absence of a lawyer or highly qualified co-juror, the other jurors would look for guidance or influence elsewhere...as they are not in a position to decide by themselves," said Anwitha.

"Yeah, from attorneys of either side and the Judge who instructs them on the law, both substantial and procedural?"

"But the problem is with them being *influenced*...unlike a professional Judge who is required to be convinced both on the law and the facts to give her decision. A lot of times, experienced and shrewd attorneys have an upper hand. They could take advantage of inexperienced or young attorneys. Only a Judge trained in law will be better able to handle such situations," Anwitha said recalling the incidents in Karnataka High Court.

"Yeah, I see what you mean," said Mia.

Anwitha was quiet.

Mia smiled and said, "You know, my International Arbitration class professor also said that many Asian legal professionals have a hard time understanding the American jury system."

"Hmm, as yet, it doesn't make any sense to me either...hope I will figure it out eventually," Anwitha said.

"Hmm,"

Mia said, "Don't worry, there are some things I'm not comfortable with the jury trial either."

"Like what?"

"Like, you never know what the jury is really thinking. Their decisions can be unpredictable often times. But I guess I'm more used to it. Like you are, to the art of driving in India...ha ha!!" Mia laughed.

"Ha ha, good analogy," laughed Anwitha.

They got up and walked to the library, to work on their assignments.

It was evening when they were finally done.

***

Anwitha reached her apartment building and opened her mailbox.

"This fills up so fast!"

There were some junk mail and a mail from the Superior Court of California, County of San Mateo.

"Hmm? What can this be?" she double checked the name and address. *"My name and address is correct. It is indeed addressed to me!"* she closed the mailbox and walked up to her apartment.

She quickly washed her face, made a cup of coffee and opened the mail from the court. It was the summons from the County Court asking her to appear for jury duty!!

Anwitha turned the page over.

Given on the back of the form were several reasons for being excused. One of them was, "Not a citizen of the United States of America."

Anwitha sighed, *"I cannot believe it is this random!!!"*

13. Nullification

"Pretty decent deal I got!" Anwitha looked around after spending an entire day setting up her newly acquired furniture in the apartment.

From Ikea, she'd got a couch, sofa chair, coffee table, twin mattress and a small table clock. She found a bed frame, bedside table, a small dining table set and television for free on craigslist.

She sat on the sofa and began to browse the TV channels. When a news channel came on, she stopped.

"Sharan keeps teasing me how I never keep myself updated of current events."

***

"Sharan had called. His wife Hema is expecting," Anwitha read the email from her mother.

She checked the time. *"It's 10 a.m., Sunday, in India. Let me call him,"* she picked up the phone.

"Hello?"

She changed her voice to make it sound like a small child and said, "Hello daddy!!"

"Who's this?"

"Naanu. Anwitha!"

"Hey! Yen samachara? Always mischief?"

"Ha Ha! Congratulations!"

"Thanks!"

"When is the baby coming?"

"In about six months."

"How is Hema?"

"She's good. Her obgyn has advised some special diet and exercise."

"Okay,"

"It's the one near your home. Doctor Priya. Recommended by our family doctor,"

"Oh! She is awesome. Has decades of experience and highly reputed. She delivered me!"

"Really?!!"

"Yes!"

"Look at how you turned out! Glad to know my wife is in good hands."

"Yes, rest assured!"

"Hmmm,"

"Mathe? How is everything in Bangalore?"

"As usual. How is your studies going on?"

"Just as you warned. Pretty intense."

"Hmmm,"

"Four months have already passed,"

"Oh, four months already? Hmm, did you finish the comparative law portion yet?"

"Yes. We have. We have our exams next week. Then there's a break until second week of January."

"Ok, great. Did you make any friends?"

"Yes, I have. Her name is Mia. She is very sweet and friendly."

"Okay good,"

"She recently passed the CalBar."

"Wow! That's great."

"Yeah,"

"Hmm, what else?"

"You know what? Although it's not a major part of my LLM studies, I'm quite intrigued by the jury system here."

"What about it?"

"I don't really get it. It's exactly like the doctor couple case you mentioned about, and I'm not able to differentiate it."

"Hmm,"

"If the facts alleged were proved, would the outcome in the doctor couple case be any different if it had occurred in California instead of India? Would it be okay if instead of one untrained, unlicensed minor boy, an untrained unlicensed adult performed the operation? Or would it be okay if instead of one adult, twelve untrained unlicensed adults performed it…?"

Anwitha was thinking aloud, "If instead of a medical case it were a legal case…instead of being supervised by professional doctors they were supervised by legal professionals…and instead of delivering a baby they were delivering a judgment!!?"

Sharan was listening quietly.

"Would the consequences be any different?"

Sharan said, "Yes. definitely! In one of the scenarios, they would be performing their bounden civic duty and are called the jury. It is an institution held sacrosanct by the people of America and a right sanctioned by their constitution."

"Not funny! I was thinking about the consequences on the society as a whole…not just legal implications Sharan!!"

"Well, you have a point. But every system has some flaws. Here in India, jury system was abolished in 1960 after K. M. Nanavati case, and we have only bench trials and bench decisions after that. Had there been a jury trial in Jessica Lall murder case, the Trial Court decision would probably be different. Manu Sharma might have been convicted by an impartial jury. Manu Sharma was able to buy out the witnesses by bribes and threats and got acquitted in the bench trial. Finally it was the people who protested it and prompted the High Court to review the verdict. Remember?"

"Yes, I remember. But Manu Sharma, the accused in Jessica Lall case, could have still waived the jury trial and insisted on a bench trial. It is the defendant's right to have a jury trial right?"

"Yes, I guess it is the defendant's right to have a trial by jury of his or her peers. You are right,"

"Yeah,"

Sharan said, "I think one famous Judge has said, I forget his name. He said that someone who submits himself to jury trial has already accepted his guilt!"

"What did he mean?"

"He meant that juries can be swayed by emotions and bias, which may help get the defendant a favorable verdict in certain cases. But a trained Judge cannot be swayed by emotions and bias. He or she will go beyond those things and stick to the technical aspects of the case. Only exceptions are probably rare cases that shock one's conscience…where they are supposed to give certain emotional aspects due consideration according to law."

"I agree. A Judge will be able to put their own personal experiences and bias aside and decide the case purely on merits."

"So if the defendant's lawyer feels they cannot win the case on merits before a Judge or the bench, they would like to take their chances with a jury of peers. It entirely depends on the emotional appeal and technicality involved in the case. So depending on those factors lawyers decide whether to go for jury or bench trial."

Anwitha was not too pleased to hear that. She said, "But that allows for forum shopping and not right. A case that cannot prevail on merits should not prevail because of its emotional appeal."

"Yes. it should not. But it happens often. Juries have convicted innocent defendants and sometimes have acquitted a guilty defendant as well, like it happened in K.M. Nanavati case."

"Hmm,"

"What can you expect? When somebody is not proficient in law, what will they decide the case by? Based on other considerations like emotions, personal experience and bias, obviously!" Anwitha said.

"Well, it is called common wisdom! Some Judges get way too technical. And Judges also make mistakes. Even against bench trials successful appeals are filed leading to reversal. You are seeing it happen in Jessica Lall case."

"True. Mistakes happen even by professionals. Still, why do you want to entrust your pregnant wife's health to an experienced and licensed doctor like Doctor Priya and not to a quack or shall I say, 'jury' doctor?!!"

"Hey!!Don't you cross examine me!!"

"Ha ha!"

"Ha ha!"

"What else?"

"Nothing, just going on."

"Hmm,"

"What was that case again, which marked the last jury trial in India?" Anwitha asked.

"State of Maharashtra vs. K.M. Nanavati."

"I don't remember studying this case during law college in India."

"It's legal significance is that it marked the end of jury trial in India. Probably it was not discussed in law college because, they thought it does not have any relevance in the era of bench trials. That's my guess."

"How do you know about the case?"

"Dad would talk about it. He had just begun his law practice when this case was tried and decided by the jury."

"What were the facts?"

"Um, the accused K.M.Nanavati was an upright naval officer charged for murdering his wife's lover. Commander Nanavati would go on long tours for months on end because of his work. When he returned after one such tour, he found his wife to be aloof. When he enquired, she confessed to having an affair with his friend, as she felt very lonely during the time her husband was away for long periods of time. The officer, on hearing of the affair, left the house immediately…apparently he went over to the friend-lover's house, shot and killed him. After the murder, he went to the police station and confessed of his crime. But subsequently in court, the confession was refuted…on the advice of the defense counsel I guess. Yet, the prosecution obviously had a strong case and the trial was a mere formality. During the trial however, there was a lot of discussion in the media…"

"By media you mean the print media and radio right, we are talking about 1960s, even television was only in one or two cities at the time and only in very affluent homes…if I'm not wrong."

"No you are not wrong. The media then was mainly radio and newspapers and magazines. But the whole nation was following the trial earnestly. Everyone seemed to empathize with the accused Commander and felt the Prem guy, the victim just got what he deserved…everyone felt the real victim of the circumstances was the Commander."

"Okay, what happened in the trial then?"

"Despite strong evidences in favour of a conviction, the jury acquitted the Commander!!"

"Hmm,"

"So it was a case of jury nullification?"

"Yes. Later in appeal, I guess the High Court overruled the acquittal…You cannot allow a jury nullification to prevail when it is in clear violation of a law passed by the legislature." Sharan said.

"Yes. In a democracy, there is a procedure to make laws or amend them. The jury can't do it in court," said Anwitha.

"Yes. It would be unfair to let twelve persons sitting in judgment of a case to undo the existing laws or make a new law simply because they don't like the law as it is. That would lead to chaos."

"And it is actually undemocratic."

"How?"

"I mean, a law is made by elected representatives, chosen by the people of a state. How can twelve random people undo such a law while deciding a case?! It is 'twelve vs. rest of the country'! How is that democratic?"

"Hmm,"

"True. I completely agree." Sharan said.

"So were these the reasons for abolishing the jury system in India?"

"Ya probably, among other reasons."

"Like what?"

"That the jurors would be susceptible to media publications and it's hard to prevent them from being influenced by the media in modern times and that personal bias and preconceived notions of the jurors are difficult to overcome."

"And this was in 1960. How about today, in the age of internet, social media, multiple news channels and what not?"

"Yeah, but in highly publicized cases the jury is sequestered and they are admonished to keep away from all outside influence."

"Hmm, do you think it is really possible to effectively sequester anyone in today's time and age?"

"It's very very hard."

"I would say almost impossible."

"Ya, it is," said Sharan. "But why are you so concerned about the American jury system?"

"Just trying to figure it out man. You know what? I got the jury summons recently! Me!"

"Oh, they must've got your information from the DMV."

"Yes. I thought so too. I recently got my state ID made."

"Hmm,"

"Can anyone afford randomness to this extent in the justice system?!"

"I see your point."

"Hmm,"

"America is a country of very smart people but their jury system doesn't make sense to me. Either I am completely stupid or missing something here."

"Hmm, you are not stupid. Neither are the Americans! Nor the Indians. Everyone is wise in their own way."

"Hmm. What, philosophy and all?"

"Becoming a dad know? That's why."

"Hmm."

"What else? It must be pretty late in the night?" he asked.

"Yes. But tomorrow is Sunday."

"What plans?"

"Planning to hike. Mia told me about this trail nearby."

"Okay!"

"Hmm,"

"Alright then, happy holidays!!"

"Thanks, happy holidays to you as well."

"Thanks. But I don't have as many holidays as you do."

"Ya I know. Just make the most of it."

"Ya will do."

"Congrats again to you and Hema."

"Thanks thanks."

"Ok then, take care."

"You too, bye."

14. The Magna Carta

"Hey, do you want to get together for lunch this long weekend? Will be asking Heidy and Heejin as well."

"Oh, its Martin Luther King Jr day," Anwitha thought, reading Mia's text.

She texted back, "Sounds great!"

Anwitha put her cell phone in the bag and walked to the library. Her favorite table was vacant. It was by the window overlooking the rear rose garden of the campus. She got her books from the shelf, placed them on the table, put her phone on vibration mode and began to work.

"I need to finish those assignments today,"

After three hours she was done. She checked the time.

It was two o'clock. *"Great! I have a couple of hours to spare,"* she browsed for some more books.

She brought about five of them to the table and began by reading the book about the origin and history of the jury system and the Magna Carta.

***

Two hours later she leaned back in the chair mulling over what she'd just read, *"Okay, now I kind of get it. The jury system signaled the birth of the first democratic institution in the European region at a time when autocratic rulers wielded absolute state power and people had no means to check that power when rulers abused it. Initially it was enshrined in the Magna Carta as the right to trial by peers...to delegate judicial powers of the King to ordinary people. Post colonization the system went to other parts of the world including Asia and America..."*

She picked up the book on the Statute of Westminster of 1275.

"...The Statute considered those who refused to submit to jury trial as refusing to stand to the Common Law of the land. It marked the beginning of the horrendous practice known as *peine forte et dure* by which recalcitrant defendants were tortured until death or until they 'consented' to a jury trial. The defendants who refused to submit to a jury were not entitled to an alternative method of trial. It was only in 1772 that peine forte et dure was officially abolished in England…"

"Hmm, good it doesn't happen anymore," she closed her laptop, re-shelved the research books, packed her things and walked out of the library.

***

Anwitha made some khichdi with rice, lentils, vegetables and spices for dinner. She put some of it and some mango pickle in her plate. As she began to eat, her cell phone buzzed.

"We'll meet for lunch on Saturday, at 12 noon in Downtown San Mateo? Heidy and Heejin cannot make it though." Mia had texted.

"Sounds good." Anwitha texted back. "I will be there."

"Great! See you. My hubby Logan will be there too."

"Great! Looking forward."

***

Next morning when Anwitha got up she had messages from Mia and several of her friends.

"Did you also feel that earthquake?!"

"There was a 2.8 earthquake. Hope you are okay."

Gopal uncle had called and left a voice mail asking if she was fine.

Anwitha thought, *"Oh my god! There was an earthquake?!!"*

She messaged all of them back, "Oh, I guess I just slept through it. Everything seems ok,"

She showered and had breakfast.

Mia had texted again, "So see you tomorrow for lunch?"

"Yes!" Anwitha replied.

"Great!"

***

Anwitha reached the place on time and walked into the Italian restaurant Mia had mentioned. Mia and her hubby were already seated at a table.

"Hey!" Mia got up and hugged Anwitha, as she approached the table.

"This is Logan," Mia said to Anwitha. "Logan, this is Anwitha."

"Hi! Nice to meet you," he smiled extending his hand to Anwitha.

She shook it and said, "Nice to meet you too!"

Logan was about five feet ten inches, had black hair, blue eyes, long sharp nose and clean shaven face.

"He's very charming. They both make a nice pair," Anwitha thought.

She sat across Mia, and placed her bag in the chair on her left side.

The waitress came and they ordered their drinks. Logan and Mia ordered wine. Anwitha said she will have water with no ice.

"So how do you like the United States of America Anwitha?" Logan asked.

"Yeah, I like it very much. I have only been in the Bay Area so far though. This place is lovely! The bay, the bridges! The woods! Even the people are very nice and friendly. They are all so diverse and highly educated too!"

"Do you miss your family?"

"I do. But, it's kind of liberating to be alone and independent!" smiled Anwitha.

"Hmm. Mixed feeling han?" Logan smiled.

Mia looked at him and smiled as well.

"So what do you do?" Anwitha asked.

"I am an Engineer," said Logan.

"Oh Okay,"

The waitress brought them their drinks. "Are you guys ready to order your lunch?" she asked.

"Yes," they said and ordered pastas of different variety.

"Okay, it will be ten minutes!" the waitress took their menu cards and left.

"So is everything okay after the earthquake at your place?" Mia asked Anwitha.

"Yes, I think. Looks like everyone woke up at night but me! Ha ha,"

"Ha ha,"

"I understand Bay Area is earthquake prone? I heard there was an earthquake last month also somewhere in the Bay Area, right?" Anwitha said.

"Yes, minor tremors happen several times a year and each time the sink pipe in our apartment bursts!!" Logan laughed.

"Yeah! The water splashed everywhere and we turned the main valve off," said Mia.

"Hmm,"

"The plumber will be there to fix it later today. The landlord just messaged," Logan said.

Anwitha said, "I'm really scared of earthquakes. I've never experienced earthquakes before. The place I lived in India, is part of the Deccan Plateau which is almost earthquake free. I don't know how I would deal with it, if I were awake!"

Logan said, "Just take your apartment key, lock the door and walk out to an open place."

"Hmm, okay."

"We used to do these drills in school all the time," Mia said.

"Hmm,"

The waitress brought the food. It was steaming hot and the aroma of cooked veggies and sauces was appetizing.

Anwitha said, "Hmm, the food smells good."

Mia and Logan said, "Yes!"

They began to eat.

"So what do you plan to do after your Masters Anwitha?" Logan asked.

"I don't know. Would like to take the California bar and then see."

"Hmm,"

"I heard the Cal Bar is very difficult."

Logan said, "I heard so too."

"But Mia passed it in the first attempt," Anwitha said looking at Mia, with pride.

"Oh, it was such a relief," Mia said. "I can lend you my bar prep materials if you want. They are only from few months ago. You can still use them for most of the subjects tested."

"Sure, thanks! I'll come and get it once our LLM exam is over."

"Okay," Mia smiled.

They had ice cream for dessert.

***

"Okay, bye now," Mia hugged Anwitha after they walked out of the restaurant.

"Shall we drop you to your home?" Logan asked Anwitha.

"Thanks, but I will take the Caltrain. I'm not going to my apartment. Just thought of exploring the city so…,"

"Oh okay! Have fun," Mia smiled. "It was good to see you."

"It was nice to see you as well. Bye," Anwitha said.

"Bye, take care," Logan smiled and waved.

***

Anwitha walked to the Caltrain station. There was a train waiting and it was hers. She boarded the train, and there were just three people sitting in that coach. She went to one of the empty rows and sat next to a window.

She took out her ipod, put on the earphones and scrolled down to Indian folk songs. She played the song *kodagona koli nungitha* as the train moved. She looked at the list she had made of the places she wanted to explore and things to do in the city. Firsherman's wharf, Cruise, Alcatraz island, Ghirardelli, Crooked street/Lombard street, Bay bridge, Golden Gate bridge, Vietnamese sandwich…

"Hmm, let's see how many I can cover today."

***

When Anwitha opened the door to her apartment at 8 p.m., she heard the phone beeping. There was a message from her mom. "Call back, something important!"

Anwitha dialed her mom's number.

"Hello," her mom answered.

"It's me. Everything okay?"

"Heard there was an earthquake there. Are you okay?!"

"Oh, how did you know?"

"Talked to Sharan. He had spoken to Gopal uncle..."

"Oh. Yes, I'm okay."

"Thank god. Next time it happens just message you are fine."

"Okay. Was that the important thing you mentioned in your voice message?"

"Yes. Tried your cell phone too but,"

"Battery died. Okay, bye now. I'm very tired. Need to rest. Are you doing okay?"

"Why, what happened? Are you eating okay?"

"No, nothing happened. I'm fine. Just that I went sightseeing in the city, so tired from that. Are you doing okay?"

"Ok, ok. Yes we are ok, bye."

"Bye,"

15. The Test

Anwitha and Mia walked out of the exam hall.

"We are done finally! Oh my god! The last few months were pretty intense!" Mia said.

"Congrats to us!!" They hugged each other.

Heidy and Heejin came running from the adjacent building. "Yay! Finally!!" they yelled and high fived Mia and Anwitha.

"Can you believe we are done with our LLM program?!!" Mia said to Anwitha as they walked inside the cafeteria on WBU campus.

"I have some units in the summer," Anwitha said. "And, I have to prepare for my bar!"

They stood in the long line to order their lunch.

"Oh, don't stress about it!"

They reached the front of the line.

"Yes, what can I get ya?"

"Rice and beans burrito for me, no meat," Anwitha said.

"Garden burger and chips for me," said Mia.

They took their plates and sat at one of the tables.

"Hmm, guess this is the last lunch we're going to have here, together?" Mia said as they began to eat.

"Yeah! It's all over so soon!"

"I know right?"

"So when do you want to come get the bar review books?" Mia asked.

"In October? After my summer program is done."

"Sure! I'll keep them all ready for you,"

"Thanks!"

"No problem."

Heidy and Heejin walked by them.

"Bye guys, see you in May, at the commencement ceremony!"

"Sure!!"

***

October 2008-

"God! It's heavy!!" Anwitha removed the box of bar review books she had picked up from Mia's house out of the cab and carried to her apartment in the elevator.

She set the box down on the breakfast counter. She opened the box and took out all the books from it and arranged them against the wall next to the sofa. When she was done, she stepped back and gazed at them. *"So many books to study...all those tests to take!"*

She had her lunch and sat down with criminal and constitutional law books.

"Sixth amendment to the Bill of rights says that in every criminal case, the defendant is entitled to a competent legal representation...if the defendant is indigent, the state shall provide one for him at its own expense..."

"This is exactly like Indian law," Anwitha noted and continued to read further.

"And a trial by impartial jury."

"Hmm, that's different, for sure."

After two hours, she took a coffee break and sat with the multiple choice MBE tests.

"A lot of the hypothetical fact patterns in this test calls for thinking like a Judge and projecting the final outcome of the case," she thought to herself after working on a few multiple choice questions.

She remembered what one of her LLM lecturers would say, *"A lawyer is required to competently and zealously represent the client's case. To do this, you will have to first predict the outcome of the case and then find a way out, if the outcome is likely to be adverse to your client. Hence the law school will train you to look at any fact pattern like a neutral Judge to spot relevant facts, issues and evidence and to discard the rest..."*

After she finished tackling the MBE questions, she realized it had taken her several minutes over the time limit.

"Oh, I should be way faster than this if I have to pass!" she reviewed her answers.

"That was not so good. I need to practice a lot."

She looked at the LLM commencement picture of herself on the side table.

"I had no problem finishing the LLM program,"

She sighed. *"Why is the bar exam so difficult?!"*

She made herself a cup of coffee and sat down on the sofa. Sipping her coffee she took the outlines for the subject of professional ethics for lawyers and began to read.

After a few minutes she felt better.

"Yes I get it. The purpose of difficult bar exam is only to ensure that legal professionals are competent and conscientious enough..."

Anwitha got up and went over to the balcony. She looked at the row of beautiful houses across the street, the green hills behind them, and the sunny sky above.

"I need to do away with my ego that I'm already a lawyer in another jurisdiction," she thought and went back inside and sat on the bar stool in the kitchen.

She took another MBE test and reviewed the results. *"Better this time, but not good enough. I need a lot more practice,"*

***

"Yes, come on in," Peter said.

"I was studying the case and found this," the law clerk said walking into Peter's office with some papers. "The middle name on this document doesn't match the name of the accused. Guess it belongs to some other file,"

"Let me see," Peter looked at it. "Oh no!"

"What?" the law clerk asked.

"This DNA evidence suggests the accused in another case was actually innocent."

"Oh!"

"The papers probably got mixed up here because the accused in both cases had the same first and last names!"

"Oh!! What happened to the accused in the other case?"

"Don't you know?! I never lost a case. The guy got convicted for kidnap and murder. He has already served seven to eight years in prison."

"Oh god! But he is innocent!"

Peter was quiet. *"How could I have forgotten about the existence of this evidence?!"* he thought.

"Shouldn't we reveal the mistake? It's *Brady* violation," the law clerk said.

"Hmm? Er, yes. We will have to. Yes. Just…leave the document here. I'll take care of it," Peter said.

The law clerk turned around and left.

***

November 2008-

Anwitha switched the television on and began to browse. Although she had bought the television a few months ago, she hadn't really used it much. She needed a break from the bar preparation that was driving her crazy. She had been studying thirteen different subjects and taken practice tests in various formats like multiple choice problems, essays, and performance tests.

Watching the news Anwitha thought, *"The news channel seems entertaining. It is so weird. Probably anything is entertaining for someone preparing for the bar!"*

"Barack Obama elected as President...," the news anchor announced. There was a re-run of one of Obama's campaign speeches on one of them. *"The guy is intelligent and a great speaker. That he is an experienced lawyer shows in the way he handles questions from the reporters,"* she changed the channel.

"Search by hundreds of volunteers for two year old Caylee Marie Anthony yielded no result. Casey Anthony, the mother of the missing child was arrested last month after being indicted by the grand jury of first degree murder, aggravated child abuse…and for providing false information to the police…"

Anwitha switched to another channel.

She listened to a panel discussing and analyzing the election results. Everyone participating in it seemed excited.

"Election of a president with African heritage, is a first in American political history! It is truly the triumph of democracy! Change has indeed come to America."

"It is historic. Hope he makes a good president," she pressed the remote button.

"An unidentified gunman indiscriminately shot and killed twenty people including children. We spoke to a few survivors and legal experts…"

Anwitha leaned back.

"The second amendment is more about preventing despotism than about the right to bear arms. Times have changed. So change the laws. Today, security of a free state is not dependent on the right to bear arms…"

"Guns for self defense?!! More innocents have died than have been saved because of gun rights," there was an ad break.

"Hmm. Didn't come across any test question on the second amendment of the US Constitution in any of the bar exams,"

After a while she switched the TV off. *"The exam is less than three months away and I have so much to study."*

***

January 2009-

It was around ten o'clock in the morning and Anwitha went out to buy some groceries. It was cold but sunny outside. It had been raining everyday during the previous week keeping everyone mostly indoors. It was refreshing to step outside and walk. Bar exam was only a few weeks away. But now she was more confident. She just needed to memorize few things in a couple of subjects.

She reached the grocery store in about twenty minutes. She noticed several shoppers congratulating each other, talking with pride about their newly elected president and of their own contribution as citizens towards making it happen.

When she returned to her apartment, she glanced at the T-shirt hung outside the door of her neighbor.

It said, "Obama my President".

"There's a general feeling of happiness since the new president took oath."

Many members of the general public interviewed on TV said it was unimaginable a few decades ago that someone with an African American heritage would be the President of America.

"Feat of modern democracy. People can actually choose their leaders from among themselves and also tell them how they want to be served," she went into her apartment and put the groceries away.

"Okay now lunch and back to studies!"

She made rice and sambar with toor daal, vegetables and spices.

"Things one has to do to become a lawyer. First law school, then bar exam…"

She put some rice and sambar on a plate and started to eat.

"It is justified I guess, to ensure prudence and rectitude."

16. Sharing Time

Anwitha arrived at the California bar exam center at Daly City a good one hour early. Hundreds of other students had arrived too and some of them were sitting on the floor and cramming at the last minute.

Few minutes before the start of the exam, the doors to the exam hall opened and the students were let in.

Anwitha went in and took her seat. She took all the items she needed for writing her bar exam in a transparent zip lock case as instructed in the communication from the state bar of California.

"Hello," a man said to her from behind.

"Hi," she turned around.

"I'm Anil Bhat," he extended his hand, smiling. He seemed about forty five years old, was slightly bald and around five feet nine inches tall.

"I'm Anwitha," she shook his hand and smiled.

"I guess this is the seat assigned to me," Anil said sitting in the chair adjacent to Anwitha's on her left.

Anwitha smiled. She didn't want to indulge in too much talk just before the start of the exam. So she began reading through the instructions on the exam hall ticket, "To keep time, only non digital watch or clock which is not bigger than 2 inches by 2 inches in dimension is permitted…NO digital clock is permitted in the exam hall…"

"Are you from India?" Anil asked.

"Yes." Anwitha said without turning her head.

"I'm from there too originally." Anil said. "But, I'm a citizen here."

Anwitha said, "Okay," and continued reading.

"I see you have the same last name as me!" he said pointing to the name written on her zip lock case.

"Oh, ya,"

"Are you from north India or south?"

Annoyed, she said, "One second, I just need to check something," and took out a pencil out of her zip lock case and pretended to highlight something on her exam ticket.

"You know there are people with that surname in both India, and also in Nepal?"

"How is that surprising?" thought Anwitha.

"There are a few Bhats in other neighboring countries too,"

"Of course, some were a part of India not so long ago…"

"You know California bar exam has the lowest pass rate in the country…?"

Anwitha was quiet.

"Even New York bar exam is very tough…"

"Oh my god, he talks so much!" she thought and simply nodded her head without taking her eyes off her paper.

"This is a very difficult bar exam. I hope I pass this time. I've already taken it thrice."

"Best of luck!" she said.

"Best of luck to you too."

"Thanks!"

She set her watch down on the table when one of the proctors began giving instructions as the other proctors distributed answer papers. It was followed by sealed question papers.

Tension filled the hall as the instructions to open the question papers were given. The students hurriedly opened the sealed covers and took the question papers out and began to write their answers.

After three hours, the morning session of that day was done. Anwitha went out, sat at a table and began having her lunch that she packed from home. Some students were still cramming for the afternoon session of the exam. Anwitha always got tensed and disturbed by last minute cramming. She just relished her idlies and relaxed. As she finished her lunch and put the box into her backpack, she saw Anil walking towards her.

"How did it go?" he asked.

"Okay I guess."

"I couldn't answer well, partly because I didn't have a watch."

"Why didn't you bring one?"

"I did bring one, but they wouldn't let me take my digital watch."

"Of course, it said clearly in the instructions, that digital ones are not allowed."

"But I didn't read."

"Hmmm,"

"Can you share your watch with me for the next exam? You may place it in the middle of the space between us on the table, so I could use it too?"

"Sure," said Anwitha thinking, *"How could he not read the instructions properly? It was stated very clearly."*

The afternoon test session began at 2.00 p.m. As Anwitha was writing her answer, she turned to look at her watch to see how much time was remaining. Anil had moved it farther from her and closer to him! She grabbed her watch and placed it midway. She noted the time to ensure she wasn't falling behind and continued writing. After a few minutes, she turned again to check her watch. It was again moved farther from her!

"Oh god! This is so distracting. I have to think of a better solution for this border problem," she noted the time in her watch and continued writing.

Half hour later everyone was out. Anwitha had Gopal uncle pick her up. When she went home, she grabbed the small ikea clock on her bedside table and put it in her backpack.

She handed the clock to Anil the next morning and said, "Here, you can have this for the rest of the bar exam!"

"Oh thanks!"

***

By 5 p.m. that evening virtually all the students were exhausted both mentally and physically.

"Still one more day to go," Anwitha thought as she walked out of the exam hall.

"How did it go?" Anil asked walking closely behind her.

"It was okay," Anwitha said.

"How did you do?"

"Okay,"

***

Next morning Anwitha woke up and got ready to attend the third day of the bar exam. She was pretty satisfied with her performance in the last two days.

"Hope I do well today too," she prayed before leaving home.

When she reached the exam center, some people were handing out flyers. They gave one to Anwitha and said, "We are a nonprofit organization providing legal aid to low income groups. We are in need of volunteers. Please give us a call after your bar exam if interested."

"Sure I'll think about it," Anwitha said and walked to the exam hall. Everybody inside the exam hall seemed happy the ordeal was going to be over that day.

"I'm sure all of them are going somewhere to party in the evening. We all deserve it," Anwitha thought.

***

The students opened the envelope at the prompt and began to answer the test.

At 5 p.m., the proctor said, "Time's up!"

Everyone put their pen down, and began clapping loudly! Anwitha joined too. Even her neighbor Anil. As the students were dismissed, Anwitha picked up her things to leave. She had a good feeling that she had performed satisfactorily.

Anil asked Anwitha, "Can I have your email? I want to keep in touch."

She said, "Sure," and gave hers and he gave his business card. It said Insurance Broker.

"You have an alternate profession huh? You don't have to really worry about the bar exam results. It does not affect your livelihood," Anwitha said.

"No but it will add to my qualification. I don't have to hire a lawyer to do some of the works concerned with my broker business."

"Okay! Best of luck."

"Hope we all pass!"

"Hope so too!"

"Whew! The exam is finally over. I'm going to watch a lot of movies," Anwitha began to walk toward the bus station. She had told Gopal uncle she will not need a ride that day.

She took the cell phone out of her bag and switched it on. Instantly it rang!

17. Varied Views

Anwitha answered the phone.

"Hi Mia!"

"Hi! Done with the bar?"

"Yep!"

"Great! Wanna get together at my place tonight for dinner? Heidy and Heejin will be there as well! They can pick you up on the way."

"Sure! Count me in."

"Actually, you can stay overnight. Logan is in Singapore on a work assignment. We can spend the day in the city or do something fun tomorrow."

"Okay! Sounds good."

***

About an hour later Heidy, Heejin and Anwitha were at Mia's apartment in Redwood City. It was on the ground floor. Mia saw them approach from the kitchen window and opened the front door.

"Hi guys!"

"Hi!!"

"Come on in!"

The girls stepped into the hallway. To the right of the hallway was the kitchen that extended to the dining area. Mia closed the door and led them along the hallway to the living room situated beyond the kitchen wall. The living room connected to the dining area.

"Nice apartment!"

"Thanks," Mia said.

"Nice aroma!"

"What's cooking? Let's help you!!"

Everyone got busy in the kitchen.

***

They placed their drinks on the coffee table and sat on the sofa with their plates.

"How did your bar exam go Anwitha?" Heidy asked.

"Went well. Fingers crossed."

"Best of luck!"

"Thanks!"

Heejin said, "What kind of law do you want to practice?"

"I want to do litigation," Anwitha said.

"I have a friend who practices criminal law. He is looking for help. Would you be interested?" Heidy said.

"Well, I am not comfortable handling jury trials. Criminal law invariably involves jury trials."

Mia looked at Anwitha and said, "Oh yeah, I remember the discussion we had about it once."

Anwitha turned to Mia and smiled.

Then turning to Heidy sitting to her right, she said, "I'm unable to convince myself that common wisdom can be a substitute for professional wisdom."

Mia said, "Hmm, professional wisdom…that's an interesting term!"

"I just made it up!!" giggled Anwitha. She said, "I feel random Judges can only render random justice. Justice is a hit or miss with the jury…not guaranteed."

Heidy said, "Well, I disagree to call the jury a set of random Judges as you put it. The jury pool is randomly picked no doubt, but each one of them is put through a rigorous screening process. Many are let go if they do not pass the process. So it is not really as random as you think."

"Oh, there is a screening process?" Anwitha said.

"Yes, for bias and preconceived notions," Mia said.

"Oh yes, I recall you telling me that," Anwitha said turning to Mia.

Heidy said, "Also, they are made aware of the relevant legal concepts affecting the case before they sit for trial, and, they work under the supervision and instructions of the Judge…"

"Hmm, I don't know how effective that is," Anwitha said, thinking about the doctor couple case.

"Despite this, if something goes wrong, one can always file an appeal to the higher court," Heidy said.

"I don't think appeal is a good enough remedy always. It costs time and money, which many litigants cannot afford," Anwitha said.

Heidy took a sip of her drink and said, "Jury system is an esteemed democratic institution that has been tried and tested for many centuries."

"Every system, no matter how esteemed, will need reforms with changing times."

"Yes," said Heejin and added, "Also is the question of accountability. A lawyer or a Judge will exercise due diligence. There is no accountability for a jury member if there is no due diligence. How many jurors are even comfortable to serve on the jury? They would rather be somewhere else."

Anwitha said, "Yes, that too. How do you ensure they will even apply their mind and act responsibly?"

"The jurors are required to take an oath, that they will conscientiously try the case and decide according to evidence," Heidy said.

"Okay, but still," Anwitha said.

"What?" Heidy asked.

"She is not convinced," Mia said smiling.

"I know they may mean well but without the necessary training how will they do well?" Anwitha said.

Heidy said, "Okay let me ask you this. Would you argue that a democratically elected government is bad because a lot of voters have no formal training in political science or that they cast their votes based on common wisdom? See now Obama has been elected as President. It's historic. Don't you see common people's wisdom in that?"

"Hmm, you make a good point there but it's debatable," Anwitha said.

Heidy took a sip of her drink and smiled.

Mia said, "Okay, I guess it's time for dessert!"

Heejin said, "I'm full!"

Heidy asked, "What's for dessert?"

Mia said, "Ice cream cake!"

"Wow! I guess I will have some!" Heejin said.

Everyone laughed.

After eating the dessert they all put the dishes in the sink.

It was almost midnight when Heidy and Heejin began to leave.

"Do you guys want to stay over?" Mia asked them.

"No. I have to pack. I'm flying back to Texas tomorrow afternoon…couldn't find a job of my choice here so joining my dad's private practice," Heidy said.

"Oh, okay, will miss you!"

"I can't either. Got an interview at San Diego. Driving there early in the morning," Heejin said, wearing her boots.

"Oh, all the best!"

"Thanks guys!"

"Anwitha you are staying over right?" Mia asked.

Anwitha said, "Yes!"

"Alright guys, bye," Heidy and Heejin said and walked out the door.

Mia said, "Bye," and closed the door.

Anwitha and Mia walked back in and sat on the sofa.

Anwitha looked at the shelf next to the television and asked, "Are those photo albums?"

"Yeah," Mia said going up to the shelf and picking up the photo albums.

"These are my wedding albums and these are from my childhood days…and these…my family and school friends," she said putting them all on the coffee table.

Anwitha began to look through them.

"Wow! Beautiful! You were the prettiest bride ever!" she said.

"Thanks! We just had a small intimate wedding in the City Hall. I couldn't afford a big wedding. Also there wasn't time to invite many people. We got married in a rush. Just my parents and Logan's aunt were there. His parents are no more…passed away when he was only seven years old, "

"Are you an only child?"

"Yes,"

"Me too,"

"Hmm,"

"May be that's why we get along so well," Mia smiled.

Anwitha smiled back.

"How did you and Logan meet Mia? If you don't mind my asking,"

"No, I don't mind," Mia said, "We met in school. At the time, his aunt was working in Florida as a teacher. He has been my first and only boyfriend since high school! I knew he was the right one for me. We dated for about six years…He proposed marriage to me within the first year of getting his job, at twenty three. And we got married as soon as I moved here few months back. What about you? Have you thought of marriage or boyfriend yet?" Mia asked.

18. Pro Bono Counsel

"Um, well, my parents are looking for a marriage alliance for me," said Anwitha.

"Oh! How does that work?" Mia asked.

Anwitha smiled and said, "Well, the parents of a prospective bride try and contact the parents of prospective grooms through someone or these days through matrimonial websites etc., and when your criteria are matched, the families meet along with the bride and the groom. In some instances horoscopes are compared as well. After that, the girl and the boy may meet separately and talk. If they like each other the parents fix the wedding, which usually involves elaborate preparations and traditional rituals."

"Oh. So the decision is taken in just one meeting between the couple?"

"No, no. Sometimes it could be more than one."

"Okay, interesting!"

"But now that you are here, how is this elaborate procedure going to take place?" Mia asked.

"I don't know. I don't worry about it so much as yet...I plan to work here for a few years and then see. I have started to look for a job."

"Hmm,"

"I know of a lawyer who is looking for help. Would you be interested?" Mia said.

"Sure! I'm interested to know more."

"Great! His name is Connor Parker and he does criminal law, but his firm has many other areas of practice, like family law, estate planning, immigration, employment law...so you can practice in the area of your interest. The firm has its offices right here in Redwood City. Connor is really nice. I've met him several times in court during work and he told me a few weeks ago that there's an opening."

"Thanks for letting me know. What's the name of the firm?"

"It's CPLaw Firm," Mia took out a page from a notepad on the shelf and wrote down the name and phone number and gave it to Anwitha.

"Thanks! Will get in touch with him."

"You are welcome."

Mia was quiet a moment and said, "I have an unsolicited advice, if you don't mind,"

"Yeah? What is it?!"

Mia said, "I think you should give marriage a serious thought. You are around twenty six now?"

"Yes,"

"Still very young, but if you find the right guy not too early to settle down. Actually, get busy and start looking now. It is a lot easier to adjust and grow with your spouse when you are young. Just my opinion."

Anwitha was quiet.

"Also, now you are not in a desperate situation, so you will make a better choice than when you are much older…"

"Hmm. guess you're right. But if anything goes wrong, I'll sue you for bad advice!!"

"Ha ha sure!! Wanna watch a movie?"

"Okay!"

***

Next morning they woke up at 9 a.m. Mia loaded the dishwasher and Anwitha made pancakes for breakfast.

"Okay. Let's hit the city! Tell me all the places you couldn't cover last time," Mia said after breakfast.

"Okay! Here is the list. I'll go get ready," Anwitha went to the bathroom.

***

The landline phone rang.

"Hello, Mia here,"

"Hi, I am told you handle pro bono cases. I'm in prison for crimes I didn't do. Can you help me...?"

"Sure, what are you serving time for?"

"Kidnap and murder but I didn't do it..."

Mia's cell phone rang. It was Logan. She texted him, "Talking to an indigent client in prison."

"Ok. Will call later."

"Thanks for understanding," she texted back and resumed talking on the landline.

***

Mia proved her excellent driving skills as she drove through the many steep yet busy streets with scenic views of the San Francisco city, the woods and the bay.

When they were on Lombard street Anwitha said, "Oh my god, I can't believe this crooked street is actually a functional street!"

"Ha ha, I know right?!" Mia laughed.

Then they took the long ride through Richmond and Golden Gate, admiring all the great architecture and finally crossed the famous and iconic landmark, the rusty red colored Golden Gate Bridge itself.

For lunch, they bought Vietnamese sandwiches from a mom and pop shop and picnicked at Crissy Field. Before heading back, they shopped at the Union Square. Anwitha bought a formal blazer and Mia purchased some tops.

***

It was late in the evening when Mia dropped Anwitha off at her apartment in San Carlos.

"Bye, had a really great time today," said Anwitha getting out of the car.

"Me too! We can visit the Japanese tea garden or hike in Muir Woods next time, I haven't been there either," Mia said.

"Sure! Sounds great. When is Logan returning?"

"Tomorrow night."

"You want to stay over at my place tonight?"

"Um, I have nothing to change into."

"I'm sure I have something that will fit you. I can make some Indian dinner for you to try."

"Okay, that sounds tempting! I'll park and come up."

"Great!"

Anwitha made some seasoned yogurt, medium spiced green moong daal curry with tomato and onions that Mia had helped chop, few rotis and some rice. They were so tired they slept soon after dinner.

19. Contemplation

"Ethics would require that we tell the court. But there will be repercussions...," Peter read the file cursorily. *"The mistake wasn't deliberate but the media might blow this out of proportion,"* he glanced at the name of the accused on the file.

He leaned back. *"Can I really rectify this without risking my prospects in the Attorney General elections...?!"*

***

After Mia left the following day, Anwitha called her mother.

"Haan, how are you?" her mom asked.

"Fine. Survived the bar exam!"

"How did you do?"

"Have done my best."

"Well that's what anyone can do."

"Hmm. How are you?"

"We are okay, so are you ready to think about marriage now?"

"Hmm,"

"What?"

"Um, okay, it depends…may be," said Anwitha awkwardly.

"Nodu Anwi, there is a nice alliance we got through your mava. The boy works in San Jose. He is a software engineer. I've emailed his photo and phone number. We've met the boy's family and the boy. They saw your photos and the boy is interested in meeting you. I'm sure you'll like him too. He returned to San Jose couple of days ago. May be you can meet with him."

Her mother paused before continuing to say, "I'm only asking you to just meet him once and see if you want to proceed."

"Okay,"

"Is everything else alright?"

"Yeah."

"Any more earthquakes?"

"No no, not where I live,"

"Okay then,"

"Okay bye,"

Anwitha hung up the phone and logged in to her laptop to check her email. There was the one her mother had sent. She saw the boy's photo. Something about his face suggested honesty. There was also an email from him.

She clicked on it.

"Hi Anwitha,

My name is Mahesh. I live in San Jose…Originally from Hyderabad.

As you may have been informed, my parents met with your family last week. I would like to meet you so we can know each other better.

Let me know and I will call you.

Bye now.

-Mahesh."

"Hmm. Pretty formal..."

She composed her response and reviewed it.

"Hi Mahesh,

Thanks for the email. Call me when you get a chance. Here's my cell phone number…bye now,

-Anwitha."

She clicked the send button and closed the laptop.

"I'm going to binge watch some movies today," she switched the TV on.

She watched a couple of movies, had late lunch around 3 p.m. and then took a nap. She woke up when her phone rang.

She picked it up and said, "Hello?"

"Hello,"

"Yes?"

"Hi this is Mahesh. Is this a good time to talk?"

"Um," it took her a couple of seconds to realize who Mahesh was.

"Hello?? Is this Anwitha?"

"Hi! Yes, this is her…!"

"Hi there. Are you busy with something?"

"Um, no, just give me a second,"

"Sure,"

She kept the phone on the nightstand and rushed to the bathroom and splashed some water on her face.

"There. Now I feel more alert," she quickly dabbed her face with the towel and went back.

"Hi, sorry about that," she said after picking up the phone.

"No problem. How are you?"

"I'm good. How are you?"

"Good too, thanks. So you live in San Carlos?"

"Yes,"

"I heard you were studying for the bar exam?"

"Yes, just finished it two days ago."

"Oh Great. So now enjoying yourself?"

"Yeah. Totally!!"

"So tell me how did you get into law? Do you like to argue a lot?"

"Well, no! I like to solve problems."

"Oh really?! I never knew lawyers actually solved problems. Ha ha, considering the kind of jokes that are made of them…"

"Oh yeah I know, I know. There are all sorts of people in all fields."

"Yes, ha ha, can't argue with that!"

They talked for about half hour interspersed with a lot of laughter.

"Can we meet tomorrow for lunch if it's okay with you?" he asked.

Anwitha was quiet.

"Okay, think it over and text me tomorrow morning." Mahesh said.

"Sure."

"Bye then,"

"Bye,"

***

Anwitha switched the TV off.

"Hmm. Wish I had something worthwhile to do right now," she got up and vacuumed the apartment and put all the bar books back in its box. *"Hope I don't need them again,"*

She cleaned her backpack and saw the flyer about the legal aid clinic inside one of the pockets.

"They seem to be working for a good cause. Until I get a job I could volunteer here for a while," she stuck it on the door of the fridge. *"I'll contact them next week."*

She had dinner and thought about the conversation she had with Mahesh. She composed an email to her mom.

She typed, "I'll be going to meet Mahesh tomorrow," and clicked send.

***

"Could you come pick me up for lunch? I don't have a car," Anwitha texted Mahesh at 8 a.m. the following day.

"Sure! Will be there around twelve," the reply came instantly.

At 11:50 a.m. the door bell rang.

20. Major Decision

Anwitha was dressed and ready. She wore blue jeans, maroon kurthi, big ear rings and very light make up.

She looked in the mirror one more time. *"Okay...,"* she went to the front door and opened it.

"Hi," she smiled.

"Hi," Mahesh smiled back.

He was around six feet, wheatish, clean shaven, had slightly broad, straight nose and brown eyes.

She locked the door and they started to walk down the stairs.

"You are more beautiful in person than in the photo," said Mahesh.

"Thanks!"

They sat in his car. "What cuisine do you want to eat?" he asked.

"Indo-chinese is okay with you?"

"Yes, you want to go anywhere in particular?"

"Do you have any place in mind?"

"There's one nice Indo-Chinese restaurant in Fremont. You want to try?"

"Sure, sounds good!"

They reached the restaurant in Fremont after half hour. They ordered veg manchurian, noodles and fried rice.

"What are your hobbies?" he asked as they waited.

"Water sports, music, dance, movies,"

"Hmm, what kind of music do you like?"

"Classical and folk music,"

"Hmm,"

"How about you, what do you do for fun?" she asked.

"I like to do everything you mentioned and I also like hiking, camping and skiing."

The food was served.

"I also like hiking and camping. Never tried skiing," said Anwitha.

"Hmm, you should try some time. You don't have to go too far for snow or ski resorts. It's only three to four hours of drive from here."

"Hmm, I will."

***

When he dropped her off at her apartment it was around 4 p.m. She said bye when he stopped the car in front of her building. He waited until she got inside the building and waved bye before driving off. She went up the stairs to her apartment thinking about him.

"Seems like a nice guy..."

She reached her apartment door and opened the lock. As soon as she went in, she heard the answering machine. She knew it was her mother. She saw the number on the phone and confirmed it was her. Not bothering to check the message, she called her mother back. She knew her mother just wanted to know how the meeting with Mahesh went.

"Hello," it was answered at the first ring.

"How did the meeting go? What do you think of the boy?"

"I think he is okay."

"Oh thank god. Finally! I'm so happy to hear that," her mom replied.

"So shall we take this matter further with his family?" her mom asked.

"Wait. Not yet…I just need to think about it a little bit."

"What do you need to think about?"

"I don't know, just…want to be very sure before I say yes."

"Okay, think it over and tell me tomorrow."

"Tomorrow?!!! No, I need more time. At least a week!"

"Okay, but try to decide as early as possible."

"Okay bye,"

"Bye,"

Anwitha sighed as she kept the phone down. *"I cannot decide under such pressure...,"* she switched the television on and tried to watch a movie but dozed off in the middle of it.

***

It was 7 p.m. when she woke up. She emailed the volunteer coordinator of the legal aid for low income groups. She also wrote to Connor Parker asking for an opportunity to interview. Because of Mia's reference she got an email response within a couple of hours. It read,

"Your resume is impressive. Please email me after you receive the bar results.

-Connor"

"Ok, he'll probably hire me if I pass the bar!"

She made plain rice for dinner and had it with yogurt and pickle as she wasn't too hungry. She watched some TV and went to sleep.

Next morning she saw a text message.

"Hi, good morning. Would like to meet you again if it's alright with you. Are you free for dinner next Saturday? Let me know. Mahesh."

"Yes. I'm free for dinner next Saturday," she replied.

***

Anwitha wore a traditional salwar kameez with a bindi and jhumka ear rings. She tied her hair up in a pony tail. Mahesh arrived around 5 p.m. to pick her up.

When she opened the door, he said, "Looking good!"

"Thanks," she smiled.

He was wearing jeans and a light blue T-shirt.

"Shall we leave?"

"Yes,"

She locked the door and they walked downstairs and sat in his car.

"Do you want to go for a walk or something before going to dinner?"

"Yes, sure."

"Crystal Springs trail?"

"Okay,"

They reached the place in about fifteen minutes.

"So how is your weekend so far?" he asked, parking the car.

"Good," she smiled. "I'm currently job hunting so there's no difference between weekdays or weekends."

"Okay. Good luck with your job search!"

"Thanks!"

They got out of the car and started to walk.

"How ambitious are you?" he said.

"Ambitious enough to want a meaningful life..."

"How do you think you can achieve it?"

"I don't know. I will have to figure out once I get married and start a family. All I know at this stage is I will need to do what is most needed in a given situation. Both career and family are essentially commitments you have taken on. I will need to choose and prioritize those commitments depending on future circumstances..."

"Hmm," said Mahesh nodding his head in agreement.

"How about you?"

"I'm ambitious as well...to have a balanced and happy life."

"Repeats what I said! Is he mocking me?"

"It is almost six, shall we walk back to the car?" he asked.

"Yes," they turned around.

"What do you want to eat?" he asked when they reached the car.

"Do you like Mediterranean?"

"Ok, there is a nice place on El Camino Real. Have you been there?"

"No, but we could try,"

They got into the car and drove to the restaurant. It was crowded and they had to wait for a few minutes to be seated.

"So where did you learn skiing?" Anwitha asked, after they got a table and placed their orders.

"In Tahoe, are you interested?"

"Yes, want to try."

"I'm sure you will pick it up."

"Thanks!"

Their food came and they began to eat.

"What are you looking for in a husband?"

"Well, apart from honesty, I would like him to support me whether I decide to pursue my career or be a stay at home mother during the years my child would need me. I don't know what I would like to do right now. As I said it would depend on future circumstances. I have seen how my mother devoted her life for me, and it has made me who I am today."

"Hmm,"

"I would like to do as good a job as her if not better. I do understand it was her choice to be a stay at home mom until I grew to be completely independent and my choice may be different. I may not want to quit my job entirely or I may actually decide to. You know…it all depends. I would like my life partner to support me in whatever decision I take and trust me enough on that."

"Okay, fair enough," said Mahesh.

"What would you want from your wife?"

"Pretty much the same things…someone honest and who can prioritize and balance her family and career commitments well."

They finished eating and the waitress cleared the table.

"What would you like for dessert?"

"I'm full actually," Anwitha said.

"Okay,"

They paid the bill and left for her place.

***

He parked the car in the parking lot of her place.

She said, "Thanks, bye!" and opened the door of the car to get out.

He got out of the car as well.

"Wait, let me walk you up to your apartment," he said.

"Okay, thanks," she said.

They walked up. After she let herself into the apartment, he said, "Okay, good night."

"Good night."

He turned around and left.

***

Next morning around ten o'clock the phone rang. It was Mahesh.

She picked it up and said, "Hi,"

"Hi, good morning," he said.

"Good morning."

"Okay, I'll be direct with the lawyer and get to the point."

There was a pause. She listened.

"After our meeting last night, I've come to a decision. I want to marry you. Will you marry me?"

"..."

"..."

"Hello???"

"Hi, er yes, I'm here," Anwitha said, thinking, *"That was fast!"*

"I know this is kind of too fast. But I'm quite clear about it. I understand if you want more time to think about it."

"Yes, I mean I need to think it over, thanks!" Anwitha said awkwardly.

"Sure, call me and let me know when you are ready. Bye now."

"Okay,"

She spent the whole day thinking about the proposal that she forgot to have lunch. She realized she was famished around 6 p.m. and made herself some instant noodles and ate. She showered and slept. In the morning she was sure about what she wanted to say.

"It's Monday morning. He will be at work. I'll call in the evening," she decided.

***

"Hi there!" he said after two rings.

"Hi"

"How are you?"

"Good."

"How are you?"

"Good too."

"Yes, tell me."

"My answer to your question yesterday is, yes."

"..."

"..."

"You will marry me?"

"..."

"Anwitha!? Are you there?"

"Yes. I…will marry you."

***

Peter picked up the file again and browsed through it.

"An innocent mix up and discovery of it at the wrong time by my staff…,this is so not fair to me…," he took one long look at the document.

"What's done is done. The man may be released on parole. That should make my staff feel better about the situation…I can't afford to be penalized for an inadvertent mistake or ruin my reputation at this stage of my career," Peter put it in the paper shredder.

He closed the folder and saw the name of the accused on it.

"Sorry buddy," he put the folder away in the drawer.

21. Integrity

The wedding date was soon finalized, and the families got busy with elaborate preparations. Anwitha emailed the invitation to all her friends.

She planned to be in India for six weeks from April first week to mid May. Mahesh was planning to arrive two days before the wedding and fly back along with Anwitha. He was currently sharing a place with a few buddies and planned to move into the apartment Anwitha was renting after they were married. The commute to his office in South Bay would not be too bad from the Peninsula region.

Anwitha called Mia and told her the news.

"Wow!! Congratulations Anwitha!!"

"Thanks! I would really love it if you can attend my wedding in India!"

"I wish I could come. But my dad is scheduled for a major surgery around the same time and I have to be there,"

"Oh ok, take care,"

"Sorry,"

"No problem. I understand,"

"Thanks for inviting! Wishing you all the best and many congratulations!"

"Thank you!"

***

Most of the couple's extended family and friends attended the wedding in April, at Bangalore. After the ceremonies that were highly condensed to suit modern times were over, the newlywed couple made the mandatory visits to the homes of close relatives and a few temples in various places across India.

Anwitha and Mahesh returned to USA in mid May with a load of presents. Quite a lot of presents were left behind as they would all not fit in the suitcases. When they reached their apartment, they experienced a great feeling of isolation although they had each other now.

***

On the Friday evening later that week, the bar exam results came out. Anwitha sat down to check the results very nervously. She went on the California Bar website, entered her particulars and clicked submit.

The page took a few seconds to load which felt like eternity. Finally the page loaded…and…

Anwitha had passed!

She heaved a sigh of relief. Most people probably reacted the same way on learning their bar results. Nobody ever jumped with joy on passing the bar. At least not at the moment they learned of the result. They either felt a great sense of relief or were overwhelmingly disappointed. Such is the humbling effect.

She went over and sat next to Mahesh in the living room. He just looked at her waiting for her to go.

She said, "I passed."

"Congrats!! I knew you would make it. My smart wifey!" he hugged her.

"Let's go out to dinner! I'll call and reserve a table," he picked up his phone.

"Okay! I'll tell the news to my friend Mia!" she got her phone and called Mia.

"Hi Anwitha! How are you?! When did you return!!?" Mia said.

"Couple days ago!"

"Wow! How's married life?"

"Great!! I have another good news!"

"Okay! I have one too! But you go first!"

"I passed the bar!"

"Congrats!!"

"Thanks!"

"That is great news indeed!"

"What's your good news?!!"

"I'm going to be a mother!"

"What?! Oh my god. That's awesome! Congrats!"

"Thanks!"

"Can't believe you are going to be a mommy soon!"

"I know! I can't either, but it's happening!!"

"When is the baby coming?"

"Early November!"

"Wow!"

"Okay, so you passed the Calbar!"

"Yeah! And you a mommy!"

"We have to celebrate! Why don't you come over tomorrow night for dinner?!"

"That will be awesome. But are you sure you want to cook…? I mean wouldn't it stress you out given your condition? We could order something from outside also or I could host instead,"

"Oh, Anwitha, I'm only pregnant! Not a patient!! I'm fine."

"Are you sure?"

"Yes! Of course, the doctor has said I need to be active and go about normal activities."

"Oh, Okay, thanks!"

"You are welcome!! See you tomorrow,"

***

Couple of hours later, Anwitha saw an email from the coordinator of the legal aid clinic. *"Oh they sent a reply to my application,"* she clicked on it.

It said, "Thanks for volunteering. Our clients need you and appreciate your pro bono services…"

***

Anwitha and Mahesh arrived at Mia's around 7 p.m. Mia and Logan had cooked a fabulous Italian dinner. Anwitha had taken some kaju katli, halwa and other Indian desserts she had brought from her recent India trip. She also took her wedding album for Mia and Logan to see. Both Mia and Logan liked the sweets and complemented on the wedding photos. After dinner they all watched a movie together and when Anwitha and Mahesh left for home, it was around 1 p.m.

***

Next morning Anwitha woke up leisurely at 10:30 a.m., made coffee and sat down with a cup to write emails to her mother and Sharan about bar exam results. Mahesh was still sleeping. She wanted to call her mother and tell the news but decided against it since it was going to be really late in India at that time and her mother would be sleeping.

After emailing her mother, Anwitha sent an email to Connor and informed him that she passed the bar. She scrolled and noticed there was an email from Anil Bhat.

"Oh it's that neighbor at the bar exam," she thought clicking on it.

"Congratulations! I saw that you passed. I couldn't make it ☹"

She replied, "Thank you. Sorry you could not make it, hope you do better next time!"

"Thanks," he replied.

She sent an email to Sharan.

"Passed the Bar. Feel so relieved!"

Pat came the reply, "Congrats!!!"

She opened her Yahoo! Messenger and typed, "Hey Sharan! Are you online?"

"Yes,"

"Working at this time?! On a Sunday?"

"Yeah. Preparing for tomorrow's trial cases. It's been crazy during the last several months."

"How is the little one?"

"Good. I hardly get to see him. I leave before he wakes up and return home after he is asleep. Every time I see him he would have developed some new skills. I would see him crawling one day and then all of a sudden he is able to stand up the next time I notice…wish I could spend more time with him."

"Hmm. Take a break Sharan. I think you are working too hard."

"Yes I know, but, there's just too much work commitments ya…you know how it is in our profession. A client is in a critical situation and we need to get a stay order from court tomorrow."

"Hmm, isn't there anyone you can delegate the matter to? Your son will soon grow up and leave."

"Hmm,"

"You will regret later for not spending enough time with him when he was little and wanted to be around you."

"Wow wow wow, where is all this advice coming from? Sounding so mature. Are you already on family way?"

"No no no. Not for some time now. We are still in the process of getting to know each other,"

"Hmmm,"

Just then, she received a reply from Connor to her email. It said, "Meet me next Wednesday at 11 a.m. at my office,"

"Hey Sharan! Guess what? Got an opportunity to interview for a job. Do you have any tips for me? You worked here a little while right?"

"Yes. Go well dressed, which you usually do. Smile, appear confident and friendly…rest I guess your resume will do. They will typically ask you questions like, tell me about yourself, where do you see yourself in five years, other questions may follow based on your answers."

"Hmm okay, thanks,"

"You're welcome,"

"What is this law firm?" he asked.

"It's called CPLaw Firm, they handle a variety of cases. My friend Mia, is the reference,"

"Great! A good reference is important. Good luck!"

"Thanks!"

"Okay, bye now."

"Bye, it was really nice to meet you and your family at my wedding. Thanks for making it Sharan."

"Of course!"
"Alright, I'll let you go. Take care."
"You too, bye."
"Bye."

***

The following day Anwitha received a letter from the California bar inviting her to the attorney swearing in ceremony where hundreds of new attorneys took oath together.

At the swearing in ceremony, she ran into many of her friends and they were all excited. The ceremony began and the legal luminaries made their little speeches. What one of the Judge speakers said resonated with many.

"Congratulations on your commendable achievement and welcome to the bar! You have now been officially recognized as having the ability to look at any legal problem rationally, without prejudices and find a practicable solution. However, with the acquiring of this license and these skills, comes great responsibility towards your community. There is a reason why you have to take the ethics tests prior to obtaining the license. It is to ensure that only the best and the most responsible ones get to practice law…Always practice ethics. Your first and foremost duty is in the advancement of justice. You have to set the best example for others to follow…"

The candidates were asked to stand up and the oath was administered. After that, the formalities of filing some forms were completed and Anwitha was officially admitted to the California State Bar.

While riding back home, Mahesh said to Anwitha, "Congrats wife!"

"Thanks! Hope I also get that job I interviewed for."

"Don't worry, everything will work out just fine."

***

They entered the apartment and heard the beep from the landline's answering machine. There was a message from CPLaw firm. She called back immediately. She was connected to Connor. He said, "Will you be able to join us from next month?"

"Yes. I will. Thank you!"

She kept the receiver down and told Mahesh, "I got the job!"

22. Innocent Indigent

Mahesh asked Anwitha, "What are you studying now?!" seeing her with a book.

"Preparing for a test!" she said.

"What??! Which test? Thought you are done with tests and exams!!"

"The test to obtain driver's license."

"Oh ok, that's going to be a tough one to pass!"

"Hey! Don't be mean!"

"Just kidding!!"

"I need to learn how to drive soon. I can't commute using public transport once I begin to start my job at CPLaw and the volunteer work. It will be too difficult."

"Okay. We will need to buy another car then."

"Yes, I want a cute small sized car."

"Sounds good."

The following week, Anwitha passed the DMV's written test and got her learners' license. She purchased a car and got her driving license two weeks later. *"Wow, I'm so thrilled to be able to drive around by myself again!"* she thought.

Connor had offered her a part time job in the immigration and family law department for twenty hours a week. She decided to work Monday through Thursday at Connor's and to volunteer for low income groups on Fridays.

***

Anwitha parked her car in the parking lot behind the legal aid for low income groups in San Mateo and walked over to the front of the building. *"Such pretty flowers,"* she thought going past the little landscape around it.

She went in and introduced herself to the clinic coordinator who gave her a quick tour of the place and showed her the location of the client interview rooms.

"Here are some instructions for you to read," she handed a packet. "Clients will be here in about half hour. You will be interviewing one of them."

"Sure, Thanks," Anwitha went into the conference room. At 11 a.m., some clients walked in. One of them was assigned to Anwitha. He was thin, had lots of grey hair and appeared to be in his mid thirties but was actually much younger. She led him to the interview room.

"Okay, please tell me how we can help you."

"I was convicted for kidnap and murder but, I did not commit the crimes…" he was barely audible.

"Hmm,"

He took a long pause and said, "I spent eight years in jail. A pro bono lawyer helped and…a Judge recently exonerated me as they found new evidence. I am now trying to get a job…"

"Sorry for what you had to go through. We will do what we can to help you get a job."

"Thank you so much."

***

Anwitha stepped out of the clinic in the evening and walked toward the parking lot. Passing by the flowerbed again she saw several butterflies. *"The butterfly couldn't happen prior to the happening of the cocoon…"*

As she drove home, she kept thinking about the interview earlier.

23. The Spy

"Can you please bring the green folder on my table to the Trial Court? I forgot. My bad. Thanks." Anwitha read the message from Connor.

"Sure," she replied and went into his office room across her cubicle.

"I'm in courtroom no...Thanks,"

"Okay. On my way."

***

Connor Parker grew up in Texas and had spent more than three decades in California after finishing his high school. He had started his law practice as a solo practitioner right out of law school which eventually became one of the top law firms in San Francisco Bay Area. He always wore a smile on his face despite the hectic schedules and the stresses of work. Everyone in the CPLaw Firm said they never once saw him lose his cool. "Just do your best and leave the rest to god," he would tell his staff and colleagues.

He was in his early fifties, five feet nine inches tall, chubby, had blue eyes and thick blonde hair.

Anwitha reached the San Mateo Superior Court with the folder.

"Hope I'm not late," she thought running up the stairs.

She went to the courtroom Connor was in and noticed their case was being called. Connor sat with their client at the defendant's table as the DA began to make his opening statements to the jury. He was looking over his shoulder, anxious.

"Just in time," thought Anwitha walking toward Connor.

Anwitha handed the folder to Connor. Connor took the folder, smiled and did a thumbs up, whispering "Thanks". Anwitha smiled back and did a thumbs up. She noticed a young intern, slim and tall, sitting at the Prosecutor's table, staring at her. When Anwitha started to smile at her, she looked away.

"How rude!" Anwitha turned around to return and saw Mia sitting in the second row. Mia waved at her discreetly. Anwitha smiled and went over and sat in the seat next to Mia's.

"Hi," whispered Mia.

"Hi," Anwitha whispered back.

"You have a trial too?" asked Anwitha.

"Yes, I'm seeking exoneration of an innocent person," she smiled.

"Oh."

"Come lets step out and talk," Mia said.

They quietly exited and sat on one of the benches a few feet away from the courtroom door in the hallway. A few seconds later the tall young intern stepped out of the courtroom. She stood beside the door and began texting on her phone.

"So when did you start working on criminal cases?" Anwitha asked Mia.

"It's part of my firm's pro bono. I'm working mainly on reversing wrongful convictions based on new evidence,"

"Okay, such a strange coincidence! I just helped a person last week who was wrongly convicted to get a job."

"Was it the one convicted for kidnap and murder?"

"Yeah."

"I worked on his case as well. In fact it was me who referred him to your clinic."

"Oh, and of all the people in the clinic I got to handle his case,"

"Yeah!!"

"What went wrong in his trial?"

"An exculpatory evidence was not produced during trial, which resulted in wrongful conviction."

"That is so unfortunate. Was it willful?"

"They said it was inadvertent, but I feel…"

"What?"

"Never mind. You know the District Attorney Mr. Peter, it was him. He got the poor man convicted."

"The Prosecutor in our case that's being heard right now?"

"Yes. I worked with him briefly as an intern. Like, very briefly. Like for four days."

Anwitha raised her eyebrows. "Only four days?!!"

"Yes. I had to quit because of sexual harassment,"

"Oh my god!"

"Yes, he would touch my hand unnecessarily when I handed him files or something…virtually under any pretext. Initially I wasn't sure but one time I went early to work and there was no one except me and one of the law clerks, a very nice guy, kind of like an elder brotherly figure.

He warned me about how a lot of interns experienced harassment. He said how he had been waiting for an opportunity to warn me about Peter since the first day I joined,"

"Unbelievable! What did you do after that?"

"I quit the next day!"

"Good thing you did! My god! How can you work in that kind of environment?!"

"I know,"

"What reason did you give?"

"Nothing. Just said quitting. I did apologize for quitting with short notice. I resigned by writing an email. He never responded to my email and he gives me the daggers every time he sees me. He can probably tell I quit because I somehow found out about his…you know," Mia gestured her hand to quote, "antecedents and tendencies," and giggled.

Anwitha giggled as well.

"Yes. He is actually a very shrewd lawyer and has hardly ever lost a case and is also politically ambitious."

Anwitha said, "Hmmm,"

"Yeah," Mia nodded.

"So how's your work?" Mia asked.

"Great."

"Thanks for finding me this job. Connor is a really nice boss," Anwitha said.

"Hey, no problem! I'm glad you like the job."

"How are you? How is the baby?" said Anwitha patting gently on Mia's tummy.

"Both fantastic!" said Mia.

The young intern walked up to them. She stood behind Mia and patted on her shoulder. Mia turned her head around, startled.

"Hi…!" the intern said, smiling.

"Oh…Hi…!" Mia said, smiling awkwardly.

The intern asked, "How are you doing?"

"Good…good…I'm doing great," Mia said, nodding her head.

"Um…how are you?" she asked.

"Good too, thanks, see ya," the intern walked ahead toward the stairs.

Mia was quiet until she was out of sight and said to Anwitha, "Oh my god! She works for Peter. I just hope she didn't overhear us!"

"Oh god! Hope not."

Mia looked worried.

Concerned, Anwitha put her hand on Mia's arm and said, "Well, no point worrying about it. If she has heard it, there is nothing we can do now. So why worry? If she hasn't heard anything, then also, why worry?"

"Hmm, true,"

"Relax, if you worry it will affect the baby."

"Yeah," Mia said and took a deep breath.

"Alright then, I need to get back to office, have a lot of work." Anwitha rose to leave.

"Okay, take care,"

"Bye."

Anwitha hugged Mia and walked towards the stairs. The young intern walked past her looking straight through her and went inside the courtroom.

"I have a strong feeling she overheard our conversation," Anwitha thought.

***

"You really need to hear what happened today," she said walking into Peter's office.

He did not look up.

The intern waited a couple of seconds.

"What are you working on?"

He said without looking up, "It's the case I told you to do research on," he picked up a pen and highlighted something in the file he was studying.

"Oh that sensational double murder case which will make us famous throughout the country?!!"

"Uh, it could also ruin my reputation if I don't get a conviction. Or at least a plea bargain," he continued working and didn't look up.

She walked up to his table and sat across him.

"There's not enough evidence against the accused. Better to plea bargain?" she said.

He nodded.

Leaning forward on the table she said, "Hmm, thought you should know. Your reputation is already at stake. That Mia girl is going around and telling everyone that you are unethical and,"

Peter looked up instantly.

She smiled.

"What?!"

"Yes,"

"Who told you?"

"No one. I know because…," she leaned back.

"Because?!!" he raised his eyebrows.

"I heard her. With my own ears. Yesterday. She was talking with that colleague of Connor's. She was telling that

Indian girl how she quit the job here because you made passes at her…"

Peter put the pen down and leaned back in his chair.

"Hmmm, I see…"

***

"Hi! how are you?" Mia said answering the call.

"Good, how are you?"

"Great! Are you still with the DA's office?"

"Yes, still with Peter," the law clerk said.

"Okay, what's up?"

"I have some info to share regarding a pro bono case you handled."

"Which one?"

"The kidnap and murder case where the wrongful conviction was reversed…"

24. Transformation

"It's October 6th today. Mia's birthday!" Anwitha thought driving to work in the morning, *"I have been so busy with work that I didn't realize I have not spoken with Mia for a long time. Will call her at lunch time to wish her."*

Around 12:30 p.m., she went to the lunch room, put her lunch box in the microwave, and pressed start. She dialed Mia's number on her phone.

Mia picked up and said, "Hi,"

"Hi Mia! Happy birthday!!"

"Thanks Anwitha…!"

"How are you? How is the little one inside you doing?"

"I'm in labor!! On the way to the hospital!!"

"Oh my god!! But…I thought your due date wasn't until…"

"Yeah! The little one decided to come out early I guess!"

"Oh! Are you okay Mia? Is Logan with you?" she asked.

The microwave beeped.

"I'm okay but nervous. Logan is in Singapore to work on a project…I called him and he is leaving right away by the first available flight."

Anwitha removed her box from the microwave.

"Singapore?!!! It is going to take him at least sixteen to eighteen hours to get here after he starts!"

"Yes. I have to do this alone till then…ugh, wait…!"

There was a long pause and Anwitha could hear Mia breathing deeply…and in pain.

Few seconds later, Mia said, "Hi!! That was another contraction!"

"Oh okay!"

"I hope I reach the hospital before the next one."

"Hmm, you are all alone!! And the baby is coming out…!"

"Yes. Called mom to let her know…but dad is unwell, so she cannot make it."

"Oh ok, wait! Are you driving yourself?!"

"No. I'm in a cab."

"Ok,"

Anwitha thought for a second and said, "Do you want me to be with you? I have no experience and am very scared, and have no idea how I can help you in this situation but do you think you can make use of me in any way?!!"

"I could use anyone right now who can be with me!"

"Ok! I'm on my way. Which hospital?" Anwitha closed the lid on her lunch box.

***

When Anwitha entered Mia's hospital room after an hour, she saw her lying down in the bed, wearing the hospital gown. She was asleep. Anwitha told the nurse she was Mia's friend and gave the nurse her name. The nurse said Mia has been resting in between contractions and was doing fine.

Anwitha sat on the chair by the window and texted Mahesh.

"In the hospital with Mia, she is in labor. Logan is out of town. May have to stay here overnight."

"Ok, no problem!" he replied instantly.

Anwitha took out her lunch box from her bag and began to eat.

After a while Mia opened her eyes.

"Hi," she smiled.

"Hi Mia! How are you feeling?"

"Excited and nervous!" she laughed.

"Haha, me too!" said Anwitha, thrilled at the prospect of being able to witness child birth. "Looks like you are getting your best birthday present ever!"

"I know, right?!! The timing is uncanny! But the baby may not come out today. We will not have the same birthday."

"Ok."

Mia said, "My obgyn has said I can achieve a natural birth. Oh, wait. I think another contraction is starting."

Mia began to breathe through it and after a couple of minutes it stopped and she relaxed.

"Oh, each time it is stronger and longer than the previous one."

"You are doing great Mia! You are so brave!"

"Every mom is!"

"I'm sure!"

Just then another contraction began.

***

The nurse was constantly coming in to check the progress.

In the night Mia was given morphine to get some good night's sleep. "This will probably be the last time you will get to sleep like this for a while," the nurse smiled.

"Okay!" Mia laughed.

"The doctor says going by the progress you are making, the baby should be out by noon tomorrow," the nurse said.

"Okay," Mia said.

The nurse said good night and left.

Mia handed her camera to Anwitha and said, "Here, tomorrow, please click lots of pictures for me!!"

"Yes, sure!" said Anwitha and clicked one of Mia's immediately. Then took a selfie of both of them. Mia went to sleep thinking, *"Hope Logan reaches here tomorrow before the baby comes,"*

***

Next morning Mia woke up around 7 a.m. looking completely fresh. Half hour later she felt the contractions again. This time they were more intense and frequent than the previous day. An hour later Mia was totally exhausted. Just then Logan walked in looking concerned and panicky.

"Hi honey," he said and went over to Mia and hugged her.

"So glad you are finally here!" she said.

Anwitha clicked a picture of the two.

Fifteen minutes later the baby was born. It was a girl! The obgyn holding the baby in her arms asked Logan, "You are cutting the cord?"

"Yes!" he was handed a pair of scissors.

As Logan cut the umbilical cord of the baby, Anwitha clicked a picture. The nurse handed the baby to Mia. She held the baby in her arms. Anwitha looked at the baby's face. The little one's eyes were closed.

Mia looked at her daughter with disbelief. *"My precious little baby!!!"* she began to cry.

Slowly the baby opened her eyes and looked at the mommy's face. Anwitha took pictures to capture the moment. Just then the baby began to cry loudly, and everyone around began to laugh and the nurse sang, "Happy birthday to you…," and everyone joined.

"…happy birthday dear little one, happy birthday to you!"

Anwitha clicked several family pictures of Mia, Logan and the little one. Around 1 p.m. she got some food for everyone to eat from the hospital cafeteria.

After lunch, Anwitha said, "Okay, I'll make a move now."

"Okay. Thanks so much," Logan and Mia both said.

"No problem! I had the most incredible experience ever today! So thank you!"

"Ha ha," said the tired couple.

"Bye, take care."

Anwitha hugged Mia and left. She was in a kind of trance. She got into the car and suddenly remembered she hadn't called her husband since the previous day. She dialed Mahesh's number.

He picked up, "Yen ayitu? Everything okay?"

She said, "Yes. It's a girl!"

"Great! Logan is back?"

"Yes. He is with her now."

"Okay,"

"Will be home in half hour."

***

Anwitha narrated the day's events to Mahesh during dinner.

He said, "You seem so enthralled!"

"Yeah. I saw a baby being born! It is a big deal!!"

"I know, I know," he smiled. "You know what? I was at the mall yesterday and there was a shooting incident just after I left!"

"Oh! It's getting far too common!"

After they ate, Anwitha cleared the table and went to the bedroom.

"I feel like I'm still in the hospital," she lied down and closed her eyes. *"They must ban guns, it's high time..."*

***

A speck of a baby moved around looking for a good place to rest in. When she found it, she slowly burrowed herself in the spot and got cozy...she grew a long cord from her navel, shaped a placenta at the other end of it and anchored herself to the womb.

As the baby grew bigger she began to push back the walls around her. The walls would not relent. She pulled the anchor off the wall, wriggled out and landed on the ground.

She saw her mother beckoning her.

The baby slowly stood up and took her first step, but tripped on the placenta and fell."Ouch!!" it hurt.

Her mom yelled, "Take that cord off. You don't need it anymore!"

The baby said, "No!!" and clutched the placenta tight.

"I want to keep my tetherball...and play with it," she tried to get back up but lost balance when the cord came in the way.

Mommy said, "See, it is going to hurt you if you want to keep it,"

The baby was stubborn. "No...!" she cried. "I'm keeping it forever!"

She lifted herself up again and began to toddle towards her mommy, dragging the 'tetherball' along on the ground.

After three steps, she tripped on it and fell on her butt.

25. Plea Bargain

The alarm buzzed, waking Anwitha up.

"Oh...that was quite a dream!" she got out of bed, showered and dressed.

It was 8:00 a.m.

"I still feel sleepy,"

She called and informed her office she would be working from home that day. There were a couple of court appearances she had, for which she asked a colleague to cover for her. Mahesh had made idlies for breakfast. She had some and went back to sleep. Couple of hours later she woke up feeling refreshed and sat with her laptop to work.

In the afternoon she got up to eat lunch when her phone buzzed.

"Just brought little Gia home," Mia had messaged with a picture of the baby in her apartment.

Anwitha replied, "Aww! So cute! How are you coping?"

"Been hectic. My folks will visit for a couple of weeks. So it will get better,"

"Great!"

Anwitha went to the kitchen and heated a couple of frozen gobi parathas for lunch. *"Gia...such a sweet name! Rhymes with Mia's too."*

She ate and put the plate in the sink and went back to work again.

Around 5 p.m., she closed her lap top. *"I'm done for today."*

She freshened up, made tea, poured some in a cup, went over to the living room and sat on the sofa. Her cell phone buzzed.

"Hey! Check out the news on channel...," another text from Mia.

Anwitha switched the TV on and went to the channel Mia had mentioned in the text message. "Latest in Bay Area news...in the recent high profile double murder case, the accused who had been denying all charges against him, has entered into a plea bargain. He will be serving twenty years in prison in exchange for pleading guilty. One of our reporters is at the Courthouse to speak to the Prosecutor, Mr. Peter Williams..."

"Oh!" Anwitha put the remote down and took a sip of her tea.

Peter appeared on the TV screen. He was accompanied by the young intern, who stood beside him, grinning. They were outside the Courthouse.

A reporter of the TV channel interviewed Peter. "Is it fair to plea bargain and not hold a trial? What if the accused is not guilty," she asked.

"Well, the accused appears guilty prima facie…we have strong evidence against him. He is sure to be convicted by the jury if there is a trial. In that event he could face the death penalty or at least life sentence."

"If there is enough evidence then why is the prosecution bargaining for a guilty plea…?" Anwitha took another sip.

"But, what if the accused is guilty in fact …shouldn't he be punished with the penalty he deserves?" the reporter asked.

"The society will have to bear the cost of prosecuting and conducting the trial and the probable cost of defending an appeal by the accused against the conviction. By plea bargaining, we have saved tons of tax payer's money. Also…sometimes the jury can be unpredictable and he may escape conviction."

"You have hardly lost a case…"

DUTY TO DELIBERATE

Peter interrupted the reporter and said, "Actually, I have never lost a case."

"Ok. I stand corrected. You have never lost a case. Either you have them convicted or they admit their guilt even before the trial."

Peter grinned, "Yes, you are right."

The reporter said, "We learned recently that in one of the cases you prosecuted, the accused was exonerated after spending years in jail for a crime he did not commit. There is allegation of official misconduct and suppression of material evidence which resulted in his wrongful conviction…what do you have to say?"

"Oh," Anwitha picked up the TV remote and upped the volume.

"Err, well I cannot comment on it at this time…but I'm sure it was a genuine error and not intentional…"

The intern appeared slightly embarrassed.

"So technically you didn't win all of your cases…"

"Well I don't agree! We may be appealing against it…thanks!"

He turned away from the reporter and walked away, followed by the intern.

"Oh…thanks for talking to us…"

The reporter turned to the camera and said, "So that was the Prosecutor denying allegations of official misconduct…over to the studio now."

The anchor appeared on the TV screen again. "Thank you. Earlier today our reporters spoke with the attorney of the exonerated…Ms. Mia Williams-Jones," They played the recorded clip.

"Wow, Mia…?!" Anwitha smiled as she saw Mia on the TV screen!

Mia was being interviewed remotely at her home.

"Can you tell our viewers about the recent exoneration of…"

"Yes, our client was exonerated after serving almost eight years in prison for crimes he did not commit…but there are many more challenges to overcome. He needs help to get re-introduced into the current society, obtain compensation for wrongful imprisonment…"

"How did this exoneration happen? What was the new evidence?"

"We were able to accomplish it through the DNA evidence. We suspect the existence of this evidence was withheld…"

"Oh?!"

"Isn't it a serious misconduct? Will there be an inquiry into this matter?"

"I think so,"

"Thank you,"

The anchor re-appeared on the TV screen. "So that was Mia Williams-Jones. We also just spoke with the Prosecutor of the case outside the Courthouse earlier today. He denied there was any official misconduct,"

Anwitha turned off the TV and called Mia.

"Hey! Just saw your interview on TV! Awesome work!"

"Thank you!"

"Wow! When did you do all this Mia, you are barely out of the hospital after giving birth…"

"Oh, I just gave the TV interview today. The work on the case was done much before, you know that case too,"

"I do? Which one?"

"It's that kidnap and murder case. Remember you helped the man get a job?"

"Oh yes,"

"The prosecution did a mix up because of which the man got wrongfully convicted. The mistake was inadvertent. But I got to know recently Peter failed to make amends even when it was brought to his attention."

"How did you find out?"

"The same law clerk who warned me against Peter told me about this as well."

"Oohk,"

"Poor man was indigent. Couldn't afford a lawyer during trial. The court appointed lawyer somehow missed the existence of favorable evidence,"

"Oh! Luckily you found the evidence to have him exonerated."

"Yep, better late than never," Mia said. "I'm invited to give a speech in a seminar in February about wrongful conviction. It is organized by the Innocence Project Org, are you interested in attending?"

"Definitely. Way to go! Gia sure has a terrific mom!"

"Ha ha, thanks."

26. Voir Dire

"Need to discuss something with you," Anwitha said, sitting next to Mahesh on the sofa.

"Okay, just give me a second," he said typing away at his laptop.

"Ok,"

Anwitha picked up her own laptop and browsed through the latest news in US and India. "Jessica Lall case: Supreme Court reserves its verdict…"

"Yes, what is it?" he asked closing his laptop.

"Hmm, would you be able to make a trip to India with me in April? Talked to amma earlier today over the phone. They want us to visit them, it has been a while."

"Hmm. Wait, let me check."

"Ok."

"Hmm. I guess so, for about three to four weeks may be."

"Okay, great."

Just then she received a text from Mia.

"Hey! The seminar on the wrongful conviction is next Thursday at 5 p.m. See you there!"

***

Anwitha finished arguing her motion and exited out of the courtroom. She saw Connor walking ahead in the hallway. She ran up to him.

Connor turned back when he sensed someone from behind was trying to catch up to him.

On seeing her, he asked, "Hey, how did that motion go?"

"Went great! Our request was accepted," Anwitha said, panting a bit.

Connor did a thumbs up as he continued walking briskly towards the courtroom.

"I plan to leave early tomorrow. Want to go attend a seminar with Mia."

"Oh sure! How is she doing?" he was walking so fast that Anwitha was literally running to catch up.

"She is doing great! Are you late for a court appearance?"

He smiled and said, "Yes, kind of, I'm conducting a *voir dire*. Do not want to make a bad first impression."

"What is that?"

"Huh!?" he turned and looked at her in a way that seemed to ask, *"How can you not know something so basic?"*

"Oh, of course. I forgot. You are not familiar with the jury system. Um, voir dire is a process by which we screen and select the jury members," he smiled.

"Oh okay," Anwitha pondered for a second. "May I come in and watch the process? Just curious," she asked.

"Sure! Why not? I think you should!" he smiled at her.

"Okay, I'll stay for some time and watch."

"Let me go see what this is all about," she thought.

Connor stopped at the courtroom and opened the door. He let Anwitha walk in first and then stepped in. He went forward and sat in his seat. Anwitha sat in one of the chairs and looked around.

The potential jurors were all huddled and seated behind the bar. There were about twenty five persons assembled there. The court staff was there and so was the Prosecutor.

The Judge arrived and everyone rose.

27. Entropy

The Judge instructed the court clerk to call out the names of the jurors from the jury pool. As their names were called out, the men and women got up and sat on the twelve jury chairs. They belonged to diverse age groups, gender and race. After twelve persons were selected, two more names were called for alternate juror positions. After they were seated, the prosecution was told to begin the voir dire.

The prosecuting attorney addressed the jurors and said, "The purpose of my questioning is not to pry or embarrass you but to look into your past and find out if there's anything that may affect how you may decide this case…"

"Have you had any unpleasant experience with the police?"

All of the potential jurors shook their head and said no.

"Have you been victims of crime?"

"No,"

"Alright,"

He turned to question juror number six, "What do you do?"

"I'm a second grade teacher."

"Okay, suppose in your class one of the kids complains that another child in the class stole their eraser, or pencil, how do you decide the dispute…"

The woman said, "Well I will talk to both kids and decide based on what they say,"

"Okay,"

He turned to Juror number five.

"You have kids?"

"Yes. I have two kids."

"Have they broken anything anytime?"

"Yes, a lot of times. And they always deny it." he smiled.

"Okay. How do you decide when you see something in your house broken and your children deny having anything to do with it?"

He said, "I would ask each of my kids straight out if they broke it or if they saw anyone do it. If I do not get a satisfactory answer then I will ask questions like where were they the whole time and things like that…"

"Okay, how would you know if they are speaking the truth?"

"Based on eye contact and body language, the confidence with which they answer…you can tell a liar. It's easy."

"Okay,"

The Prosecutor proceeded to explain legal technicalities like 'circumstantial evidence' and 'intent' to the jury panel. He asked them if they would understand it and if they can infer 'intent from the circumstances or circumstantial evidence'.

They all said "Yes,"

Then he proceeded to explain the term 'reasonable doubt', "…as the term implies, it is a doubt based on reason, a doubt for which you can give a reason. It is not a fanciful doubt, nor a whimsical doubt, nor a doubt based on conjecture. It is such a doubt as would cause a juror, after a careful and impartial consideration of all the evidence, to be so undecided that the juror cannot say that he or she has an abiding conviction of the defendant's guilt…"

He paused, turned a page of his notes over and continued.

"This is a murder trial…and there may be graphic pictures used as evidence…would you be okay to look at graphic pictures? Have you ever had the chance to look at graphic pictures before?"

Two ladies and one man raised their hand.

"I'm sorry. But I get very distressed and disturbed by graphic pictures," one of them said.

"Same here your honor," other two said.

"They may be excused your honor,"

"Juror number three, ten and twelve may be excused," the Judge said.

The clerk randomly picked three other names from the basket to replace the excused jurors.

She announced, "Juror number three, Anil Bhat,"

As he stood up and walked he looked at Anwitha and smiled. Anwitha recognized him instantly! He was the guy who had sat next to her in the bar exam! She remembered he had subsequently emailed to her that he failed the bar.

"He is now going to be selected to Judge a case?" she thought. *"He is not considered qualified to represent a client as a lawyer but is qualified to Judge a case?!!"*

Anil Bhat sat down in the place of the juror excused before him.

He was followed by two more replacements.

The Prosecutor turned to Anil Bhat and asked him, "What do you do for a living?"

"Insurance broker."

"Are you aware of what this case may entail?"

"Yes."

"You are confident that you can use your common sense and wisdom to decide this case?"

"Sure I can!"

After a while, it was Connor's turn. He started his voir dire in a much similar way. "My questioning is not to pry or to embarrass you but to help ascertain if there is anything in your background…"

After asking questions on their backgrounds and life experiences, Connor began to familiarize the jury with legal terms and concepts just like the Prosecutor.

"Every defendant in a criminal case is presumed to be innocent. You should not assume that the defendant is guilty because he is on trial. The presumption of innocence remains with the defendant throughout the trial unless and until he is proven guilty beyond a reasonable doubt…"

DUTY TO DELIBERATE

Anwitha rose and walked out of the courtroom. *"Is this the jury screening process everyone's talking about?!"*

She took the stairs down to the parking lot, got into her car and began to drive back.

"So...they will be given a quick crash course in criminal jurisprudence before they can sit in judgment of a murder trial!? They are going to ascertain if a witness is lying based on their body language!? It may be possible sometimes for the jury to detect lies correctly but is it by reliable methods...?! It is possible for a witness to sound genuine if they have sufficiently practiced to say something with enough conviction. Is it okay to Judge a witness testimony based on instincts and guesses?! How do we know these jurors are not biased in the first place. They may have bias and not be aware of it...can't believe people actually submit their fate to the jury!"

***

She made beetroot sabzi and sambar with cucumber, tomato and toor dal for dinner. After eating she brushed her teeth and got ready to sleep. Seeing Mahesh still working on his laptop, she went and sat beside him on the sofa with her own laptop.

"What are you working on?" she asked.

"I have to interview some applicants for a junior engineer's post tomorrow. Just going through their resumes. We have an urgent need to fill the vacancy,"

"Hmmm, hope you find a good candidate," she began her own research.

"Thanks. Not sleeping yet tonight?" he asked.

"I have some nagging questions I needed answers to."

"What questions?"

"It's about the jury selection process called voir dire…many tips by experts to lawyers conducting voir dire are like, 'Make them feel important. See who are friends or might vote together, give them undivided attention and make a good impression…' you know, sounds like many jurors might actually decide a case based on how they like an attorney, and not on facts,"

Mahesh was listening intently.

Anwitha said, "A Judge will go by evidence…and so even a bad or inexperienced attorney cannot damage a client's case as much."

Mahesh smiled and nodded, "Hmm, you worry so much, what can you do about it?"

DUTY TO DELIBERATE 237

"I don't know. I don't get it and it makes me uncomfortable."

"Sorry to bother you," she said.

"No no, it's okay,"

After half hour she said, "Okay, I'm going to sleep," and walked to the bedroom.

"Good night,"

Anwitha lied down on the bed, pulled the comforter over her and turned off the lights.

***

Soon, she found herself in the courtroom she had been in earlier and was conducting voir dire.

"Have you or any of your friends or family had any issues with their car any time?" Anwitha asked.

"Yes. many different times." answered one potential juror.

"Can you tell me of any one instance?"

"Yes. Two weeks ago, I was riding with my friend in her car and it suddenly began to make weird sounds. She pulled over and called the insurance and they sent a professional who came and fixed it."

"Okay. Did your friend ask you to fix it, before calling the insurance company?"

"No. My friend knows I know nothing about cars to be able to fix issues like that.

Even if she wanted me to, I wouldn't do it. I would have messed it up more and put us and others in danger, ha ha," the lady laughed.

"Okay, do you have any background in law?"

"No."

"But you are confident of judging this murder trial?"

"Um, yes, I think I have common wisdom."

"Thanks ma'm!"

Anwitha addressed the entire panel of potential jurors again.

"Any plumbing issue recently in any of your homes?"

Another person raised his hand and said, "I did in my home recently. There was a leak under the kitchen sink. and I called the plumber. He fixed it by installing a new aerator for four hundred dollars,"

"Why didn't you fix it yourself and save four hundred dollars?"

"I wasn't sure I could do it."

"Do you think you can judge a murder case?"

"Yes."

"How can you be so sure?"

"A lot of my peers and friends have done it. So have I, in the past. All it takes is common sense."

"Thanks," Anwitha turned to another potential juror. He looked like Mahesh.

"What do you do for a living?"

"Computer engineer and entrepreneur. I'm a CEO of a Software Company."

"Okay. Can you tell me what is the process of hiring new employees or for promotion in your company?"

"I leave it to the HR or the departmental heads that have the expertise in the area. Generally we hire based on educational qualifications, work experience in the relevant area. More important the position, more thorough is the screening process."

"Okay."

"Would you hire a person with a Phd in computer science for a post in the department of finance?" she asked.

"No," he paused before elaborating. "Not if he or she has no experience relevant to the post concerned,"

"Okay. Would you hire a lawyer to the post of an engineer?"

"No."

"Why?"

"Because a lawyer cannot do the job of an engineer."

"Would you hire twelve lawyers to the post of an engineer?"

"No."

"Why?"

"Same reason."

"Would you hire a group of twelve people with various qualifications like, doctor, financier, Judge, lawyer etc, but no engineer to the post of an engineer?"

"No, none of them can do the job either individually or as a group in collaboration! Only an engineer can be an engineer."

"Hmm, similarly, is it correct then, to say, that only a doctor can be a doctor, plumber a plumber, lawyer a lawyer, Judge a Judge?!"

"Yes,"

"Thanks,"

Anwitha turned to the Judge and submitted, "Your honor, none of these potential jurors are qualified to judge my client's case. I refuse to submit the fate of my client to all these ladies and gentlemen, who I'm sure are very nice and genuine people and may have good intentions, however, they may judge based on body language and surmises which are many times not reliable.

They may be instructed by your honor on the law and evidence, but I believe they will not be able to deliver justice simply because of lack of training and experience. Common sense and common wisdom is not enough to judge a case in a court of law if it is not enough to become a Judge, if it is not enough to become a lawyer, or a paralegal, or a doctor, or a teacher, or a banker, or a plumber, or an engineer, or a nurse, or a ..."

She paused, suddenly realizing the Judge, the opposing attorney, the court clerks, the typist and everyone else in the courtroom was staring at her, nonplussed!!

28. Stormy Seminar

Anwitha arrived at the venue of the seminar a few minutes early. The parking lot was pretty empty.

She didn't see Mia's car.

"Just arrived," she texted Mia and noticed Peter drive into the parking lot. The intern was with him in the passenger seat.

"Oh! Didn't know they would be here as well," Anwitha thought.

Her phone rang.

"Hey Mia!" she answered.

"Hey Anwitha, I'm on the way. The nanny fell sick and cancelled in the last minute. So I have to bring Gia with me today."

Peter and his intern got out of the car and walked towards the conference room.

"No problem Mia! I can babysit her!"

"Thank you!"

"Sure, see you soon!"

"Ok,"

***

When Anwitha went to the conference room, quite a few people had arrived and were networking. The intern was sitting in the middle of the first row and texting someone on the phone. Anwitha walked in and sat in the second row. There was a booklet on each chair, with program details and introduction about the panelists and the work of the Innocence Project.

On the stage was the seating for the panelists with table cards displaying their respective names…Mia, Peter, Director of the Innocence Project and the moderator/MC.

Anwitha read the booklet detailing the statistics about proven wrongful convictions in Northern California.

"Three hundred and sixty five convicts exonerated pursuant to DNA evidence. About forty five pled guilty to crimes they did not commit…"

Just then Mia walked in with Gia.

"Hey!"

"Hi there, both of you!"

Gia stared at Anwitha.

"Could you hold her a bit, just need to go over my speech," Mia asked.

"Yeah sure,"

Mia placed Gia on Anwitha's lap.

"I couldn't get any alternative nanny to baby sit and Logan is out of town…as usual."

"Okay,"

Gia looked around curiously.

"Here's her bag with some snacks and toys, if needed,"

"Okay," Anwitha took the bag and placed it in the chair next to her's.

Mia went over to the first row and began to review her speech. Peter saw Mia. With his gaze fixated on her, he went over and sat in the aisle seat across her. Mia felt someone glaring at her and turned her head.

He smiled and said, "Hi!"

She said, "Uh, hi,"

Couple of seconds later she got up and sat next to Anwitha in the second row.

"My god, he is so creepy," she whispered to Anwitha.

Anwitha nodded.

The room was now filled with people. The Director of the Innocence Project and the moderator had arrived.

Peter kept staring at Mia. She was busy reviewing her notes for the speech. He looked away as Anwitha looked at him.

"I think you will soon be called to take your seat on the stage Mia," Anwitha whispered.

"Ok," Mia took her papers and went over to the first row.

The program began promptly at 7 p.m.

After a brief introduction by the moderator, all the panelists took their seats on the stage. They were asked to address the gathering.

The Director of the Innocence Project spoke first.

"Thanks everyone for coming today…the topic of discussion today is wrongful convictions and measures to prevent them. The statistics of wrongful convictions is appalling…we can prevent this from happening by selecting smart, responsible and unbiased jury members who can properly analyze evidence…"

"Better still, let only those who are trained for the job do it," Anwitha was thinking.

"The next speaker is Mia Williams-Jones," the moderator announced.

Mia went over to the lectern to speak. Gia squealed. Everyone turned in her direction and smiled, except Peter.

Mia began her speech.

"Hello everyone…why is it important to prevent wrongful convictions? Because it is unfair. In many cases it does twofold injustice. An innocent suffers while the real culprit is not caught and it destroys the faith of the public in the judiciary. In hundreds of cases, innocents have served long sentences in prison sometimes for decades…for crimes they did not commit. And even if they are exonerated because of new evidence, it is hard to erase the blemish or the label of a criminal off their names and records. It is hard for them to return to the society and resume their life…," everyone including Gia was listening attentively.

"…this country's criminal jurisprudence is based on the principle that no innocent shall be punished even if a hundred guilty men escape…however the statistics of wrongful convictions show that accused is presumed guilty in a lot of cases. This could happen for various reasons. Either because of misguided jury, biased jury, overzealous prosecution, pressure to just hold some one accountable when there is a crime or tragedy…or seeking fame through sensationalizing certain cases," Mia turned her head and looked at Peter.

Peter looked away and clenched his teeth.

She turned to the audience and continued. "Or due to indiscriminate reporting by the media…"

Peter made some notes on his little notepad. There was loud applause when Mia concluded.

Peter's name was announced.

He went to the lectern and adjusted the mike to his height.

"Hello everyone," he began.

Mia was looking down at her notes.

"In criminal prosecution proof beyond all reasonable doubt is required for a conviction. The jury is always instructed about this highest standard of proof in the beginning of the trial and that the entire burden of providing this proof is on the prosecution. The defense team need not say anything to prove their innocence. Just as Ms. Mia pointed out here, the accused is indeed presumed innocent until proven guilty," he paused and smiled sarcastically.

"Hence, if a guilty verdict results, it means that there really was no reasonable doubt about the guilt. It means that the prosecution established the guilt of the accused beyond all reasonable doubt shifting the burden on the defense to simply create a reasonable doubt. If there have been wrongful convictions as alleged, it is because the defense didn't do their job well in creating that reasonable doubt after the prosecution established the guilt," Peter said, looking at Mia.

Anwitha was thinking, *"Hmm, reasonable doubt, reasonable person standard…how about a reasonable jury?"*

"The job of the prosecution is to prosecute. The job of the defense is to defend. The job of the jury is to give an unbiased verdict based on evidence. The jury members are picked by both the defense and the prosecution. Hence the jury cannot be blamed for bias either. If you do a good job, you win. If not, you don't, since," Peter paused and drank some water.

"That is the problem…justice should not depend on who can afford a better lawyer. Lawyers' job is to assist the court to arrive at the truth. But, the one sitting in judgment should possess the capacity to arrive at the truth independently on their own,"

"…there have been many wrongful acquittals as well by the jury. Remember the controversial OJ Simpson case?…"

DUTY TO DELIBERATE

"I would agree with him here."

"...thank you!" he concluded after speaking for about thirty minutes.

There was a round of applause.

The moderator went back to the lectern and said, "So we come to the end of today's discussion. Does anyone have any questions for the panelists?"

Anwitha raised her hand. The moderator said, "Yes?"

"I have a question to the Director of the Innocence Project."

The Director turned to her and said, "Yes?"

"In all of these cases of wrongful convictions, was the trial by jury or the Judge?"

"It was a jury verdict, in most of these cases,"

"Thanks,"

"Any more questions?"

Someone else raised their hand.

"My question is to Mr. Peter Williams."

"Yes?" said Peter.

"A good lawyer including a prosecutor cannot violate ethics to win a case. There are reports about violation of ethics by your office which resulted in conviction of innocents in certain cases. What do you have to say to that?"

Peter said, "There is no truth to those allegations…"

Mia looked at Anwitha and smiled.

Peter looked at Mia sitting next to him and said, "…some people blame others for their inefficiency."

The intern scoffed, staring at Mia.

Mia was very angry.

She picked up the mike and said to the lady who asked the question, "I deny that the defense has been inefficient in the cases you are talking about and I do not agree with the contention that a wrongful conviction results solely because of inefficient defense…it has happened due to misconduct by the prosecution. Anyways, there will be an enquiry into the matter by a neutral body. Let's wait for the enquiry report. The truth will be revealed soon."

The lady smiled, "Thank you,"

Finally the moderator concluded the program by saying, "Thanks everyone for making time and coming. Thanks all the speakers for your insights…everyone, please have dinner before leaving. Thanks again, have a good night."

Peter rushed out immediately and the intern followed him. Mia walked over to Anwitha. Seeing Gia asleep in Anwitha's lap, Mia said, "Oh, you are a natural."

"Me? Oh, I did nothing. She is such a co-operative baby,"

Mia smiled. "Okay. Let me go get dinner for both of us."

"Sure,"

Ten minutes later Mia was back with two plates of vegetable salad, pasta and bread. She gave one to Anwitha and placed the other on a chair.

"Let me hold her," Mia gently took Gia and held her on her lap.

Eating her pasta with the other hand she said, "Do you know? Of the six cases of wrongful convictions that I have worked on, five were highly reported in the media…and they had Peter as the Prosecutor!"

29. Incongruity

"Careful!" the intern yelled as Peter braked suddenly to avoid hitting a car in front of his.

Peter sighed. The traffic lights turned red.

The intern knew what was bothering him. She added fuel to the fire.

"That Mia girl is making allegations that we committed official misconduct which resulted in jail time for her client. All TV channels are reporting it," she said.

"Yes I know. She will regret it," he said.

The lights turned green. He pressed on the accelerator.

"Someone so junior is challenging me?!" he said.

"And so publicly!" she said.

"I will get her someday."

The intern smiled.

***

Anwitha and Mia finished their dinner and began to walk to the parking lot.

"Why don't you come over to my house some time? I'm planning to take a break from work for a couple of months," Mia said.

"Yes sure, we will be going to India for a month. Will visit you once before that,"

"Oh great! You are going to visit your folks!! Yes, we have to meet before you leave,"

They reached Mia's car. Anwitha waited for her to put Gia in the car seat.

"Bye!!" Anwitha said, as Mia sat in the driver's seat.

"Bye, so I'll see you soon," Mia said starting the car.

"Yes, I will text you."

"Sure. I'm absolutely free from next week!"

"Ok,"

Mia pulled out of the parking lot and Anwitha walked to her car.

Anwitha's phone rang. It was Mahesh. She picked it up and said, "Hi."

"I will be late today. Are you home yet?"

"No not yet. Just leaving."

"Oh. I can pick up something for dinner on my way. Chinese okay?"

"Okay. I already ate. I'm good."

"You may get hungry again by then."

***

"The chow mein was really good," Anwitha said, clearing the table.

Mahesh smiled, "Yes, I knew you would love it! That's why ordered for two."

She went over to the living room and sat next to Mahesh on the sofa. "What are you working on?" she asked.

"It's that junior engineer's vacancy I told you about."

"Oh yeah. Did you hire anyone?"

"No. None of the applicants have the necessary qualification or experience…"

"Hmm, they all may qualify to be jurors though,"

"Ha ha, yes, I see the irony."

"So what are your options now?"

"Either hire and train one of them…if possible, or outsource,"

"Hmm, hope you find a good solution."

"Thanks," Mahesh turned to her. "Want to take a short vacation next weekend to Tahoe?" he asked.

"Sure!!"

***

Anwitha stared at the enchanting snowy hills at Tahoe standing at the balcony of their hotel room. She hadn't experienced such cold ever in her life. It was the first time she had seen snow. Having grown up in the very tropical southern India, she wanted to visit the Himalayas in north Indian region during winter but never got a chance to do it.

Mahesh wanted to ski so they both took the gondolas up to the ski resort located on the top of the mountains. Anwitha got off at the resort while Mahesh took the lifts and went further up the slopes to ski.

"See you in the evening," he said before leaving.

Anwitha registered for a three hour session of ski lessons along with a group of other beginners. After she was done, she went into the resort to eat. The resort was over crowded as it was the only place that offered any shelter or food at that altitude. She bought hot coffee and French fries and looked for a place to sit. All seats were taken and finding a place to sit was like playing musical chairs. She stood next to a window and began to drink her coffee, watching the skiers out on the slopes. About half hour later a seat near the window where she stood became vacant. She sat down and began to eat her French fries.

She suddenly noticed that the intern who worked with Peter was sitting at the table across her's.

Anwitha smiled and waved "Hi."

She looked up at Anwitha and seemed surprised.

"Helloooo," she said.

"You don't ski?" she asked Anwitha.

"I did. Well, just took my lessons today. Not so seasoned but loved it,"

"Oh okay,"

"How about you?"

"No, I am not that athletic. Also, I can barely tolerate this cold. I like to just stay cozy indoors and watch. It's more enjoyable to see this view when you are comfortable in a warm place," she took a bite of her burger.

"Hmmm, I guess many people do that," Anwitha said noticing the clean boots of some of the people there, including the knee high boots that the intern was wearing.

"Yes! Some of my friends are out there skiing. But I come every year and spend time here, watching them do their stuff out there!" she drank the water from her glass.

Anwitha noticed there were about four ice cubes in her glass. The intern emptied the glass and threw it in the trash can.

"Hmm, that was a heavy lunch. Alright, it was nice seeing you," she pulled her cap down over her ears and walked towards the restroom.

"Yeah, likewise," Anwitha took a sip of her coffee. *"She looks cute in those boots, puffy jacket and hat,"* she took another sip.

Anwitha and looked at the skiers out on the slopes and tried to spot Mahesh. Few minutes later, she went to the restroom. It was crowded as well. She stood behind the long line and within seconds it grew even longer behind her. When she got to step into the restroom, the intern was washing her hands. She turned and saw Anwitha.

"Oh, we meet again," she said.

"Yep."

"Feels so good to wash your hands with hot water on a cold day!!" she said drying her hands with a paper towel.

Anwitha smiled, thinking, *"Funny how she prefers warm water for washing hands, covers herself from head to toe because it is cold but didn't mind drinking ice cold water at the same time!!"*

30. Crusader

"Hi Mia!"

"Hi Anwitha! Thanks for calling. Long time no see! How have you been?"

"Great! How are you and the baby?"

"Both of us doing great. I have quit work for a while…just wanted to spend all my time with my little one."

"Awesome! That's a good decision!"

"Yeah!"

"So having loads of fun with the baby huh?"

"Oh yeah! I'm thoroughly enjoying my time with my baby! I have absolutely no concept of time these days!" she sounded really ecstatic.

"Ha ha, ok. So I called to ask if I can come over today around one o'clock?"

"Yeah sure. Anytime you are free! Oh! Anwitha, I got to go! She's hungry. So I'll see you later today!"

***

Anwitha rang the doorbell.

Mia opened the door and smiled, "Hi!! So good to see you!"

She hugged Anwitha.

"Good to see you too!" Anwitha hugged her back.

"Here you are," Anwitha handed her a bag.

"Oh, what are these?!"

"A pair of onesies and a hooded towel for the little one."

"Oh thanks! Come on in."

She stepped inside.

Mia closed the door and asked, "Care for some coffee?"

"No, I'm good."

"Um, how about cookies?"

"Okay. I'll have some cookies,"

Mia went to the kitchen and took out a box of chocolate chip cookies and handed to Anwitha.

"Thanks."

Mia poured water into two glasses.

"Come let's sit here," she said walking to the living room with the glasses.

Anwitha followed her. There were toys everywhere in the living room. On the floor, on the furniture. She smiled at the sight.

"Sorry about the mess," Mia said.

"Oh no, I love it like this…signs of having a bundle of joy at home. Makes me happy!!"

"Ha ha you are so kind. Wait, let me make some space for you to sit down,"

Mia placed the glasses on the coffee table and removed some of the toys lying on the sofa.

"Here," she said.

"Thanks!" Anwitha sat down.

"Is she sleeping? It is so quiet," she asked.

"Yeah, it's her morning nap. She'll wake up in a bit," Mia sat next to her.

"You look good,"

"Thanks. I guess it's the joy of motherhood!" Mia giggled.

"Ha ha, yeah! It shows,"

"Oh thank you, how are you doing? How is work?"

"Work is great! Learning something new every day…got to watch the voir dire recently,"

"Oh you did? What do you think of it?"

"I'm of the opinion that the jury system needs a lot of reformation. You know, I saw a failed bar examinee being selected as a jury member." Anwitha took a bite of the cookie and said, "Someone is disallowed to represent a client as an attorney but allowed to judge a case as a juror. Do you see the irony Mia…why have the bar exam even?"

"I see your point. It is frightful how many innocents get wrongfully convicted by the jury. You know, in so many cases people who were sentenced to die were exonerated later?"

"Oh?!"

"I'm sure the scenario would be different if they had gone for bench trials instead. I personally would not want a jury to decide my fate either, if there ever was a case against me!"

"God forbid," Anwitha laughed.

"There may also be wrongful acquittals many times, but I guess wrongful conviction is a bigger tragedy," she said.

Mia said, "Yes. Jury trial as a matter of rule is not something I endorse either. I find it easier to convince a Judge than a jury. Someone who sits in the juror seat would come to me to consult on a legal problem if they had one, because they do not have expertise in resolving that issue. So, how can they decide somebody else's legal problem?"

"Exactly! But many people in America believe in the jury system," Anwitha said.

"Well, many people in America also believe in gun rights despite so many mass murders!"

Mia picked up a cookie, took a bite and said, "I know the two issues are poles apart but they both deeply affect people's lives. We need serious reformation regarding both of these matters."

"Hmm,"

Anwitha picked up her glass of water and drank some.

"I think people just get attached to something familiar and cannot let go. They simply refuse to see change is necessary,"

"Yes, I agree," Anwitha put the glass back on the coffee table.

"Some more cookies?"

"No, thanks, I'm done,"

"Ok, I need to have some coffee now, you want to have some?" Mia said.

"Sure."

Mia went to the kitchen and began to make coffee.

"So when are you planning to resume work?" Anwitha asked, sitting at the dining table adjacent to the kitchen.

"In a couple of months. Will work part-time and mostly from home."

"That's good,"

"I have to prepare for this investigation into the misconduct by the prosecution which caused the poor innocent man to go to prison for nothing."

"Oh, the one in which Peter is involved?"

"Yep!"

"Just hope she won't get hurt for her activism," Anwitha thought.

"What?" Mia asked.

"Nothing,"

"I mean, these are the causes that really matter. Rest is luxury litigation, right?"

"Hmm,"

Gia began to cry.

"Oh, she woke up. Excuse me, here's your coffee. I'll be back in a minute," Mia handed the coffee mug and went to the bedroom to attend to the baby.

"Okay," Anwitha took her mug and went to the living room.

Few minutes later Mia returned with Gia.

"Helloooo!! Look who's here!!" Anwitha grabbed Gia's hand. Gia giggled when Anwitha shook her hand gently.

"Aww, ha ha!" Anwitha laughed. "She has grown so much since the last time I saw her. Is she six months old now?"

"Yep,"

"Here, come to me for some time!!"

Anwitha put the coffee cup away and took Gia and held her in her lap. Gia quietly stared at Anwitha's face and began to examine it carefully. Then she extended her hand and touched Anwitha's nose. Anwitha laughed and Gia smiled.

Mia said, "She really likes you!!"

Anwitha said, "Yeah! We both like each other!! Don't we?"

Gia laughed.

"Ohhh, she is so cute. Looks a lot like you."

"Thanks!"

Anwitha picked up a rattler off the floor and began to play with Gia.

Mia smiled, "You are so good with her! While you are here, let me clean up a bit , if you don't mind," and began to pick up the toys off the floor.

"I don't mind but why bother, she is going to play and mess up again anyways, have your coffee and relax!"

"Yes, but I just need to clean this place. Because of the toys lying on the floor all the time, I hardly get to vacuum. I'm just too tired in the evening when Logan's home."

"Oh okay, sure no problem!"

Mia quickly put all the toys in a storage box and vacuumed the floor.

"Okay. That looks so much better! Just ten minutes of uninterrupted cleaning."

"You are a champ!"

"Please have your coffee. Let me take her," Mia picked up Gia and went to the kitchen and got her own coffee mug.

"When are you leaving to India?" she asked sitting down.

"Mid April," Anwitha said, drinking her coffee.

"Okay,"

"Looking forward to meet everyone. We have a lot of invites to visit from friends and relatives there,"

"Hmm, hope you have a good time!"

"Thanks,"

"Ok, I need to leave now," Anwitha said looking at the clock.

"Alright, thanks for coming by,"

"Oh, it was good to see you both! And chat with you."

"Logan said we can plan something after you guys are back from India."

"Yeah, that will be great!" Anwitha said getting up. "Here, let me put these back for you," Anwitha put the mugs and glasses in the sink and the cookie box in a drawer.

"Thanks dear,"

"Take care you two!"

"You too."

Anwitha walked to the front door. Mia carried Gia and followed.

"She will have grown so much more by the time I see her next," Anwitha tickled Gia on the tummy.

Gia laughed.

"Oh yeah!!" Mia said.

"Bye," Anwitha put on her shoes, opened the door and stepped out.

Mia stood in the doorway, waved and said, "Bye".

Gia waved her hand and said, "Aiye…"

"Ha ha, Byeee!!" Anwitha walked to her car.

31. Peers for Peers

Mahesh ate his dinner and sat beside Anwitha on the sofa. "I'm done with all the packing," he said.

"Okay...," Anwitha said.

"Supreme Court of India to pronounce its verdict on Monday in...," she closed the laptop. *"Hmm."*

He said, "There's a small change in plans for tomorrow,"

"You know about Jessica Lall murder case right?"

"What? Oh that case. I kind of remember vaguely. It was about a murder sometime in 1999, a model was killed in Delhi by a politician's son?"

"Right."

"Yes, I think a few of my friends and cousins took part in some protests against a court judgment in that case."

"Hmm,"

"I was living in the US at the time."

"Yes, the protests happened sometime in March 2006. People all over India had come together…"

"Why was she killed?"

"Who Jessica Lall? Because she refused to serve a drink to the accused, his name is Manu Sharma. It made him mad."

"And?"

"He shot and killed her, right there."

"What?!"

"Yeah, that's what happened according to several witnesses who were no ordinary citizens. They were very famous people holding important positions…one of them I think was a senior police official as well,"

"How did the murderer get away then?"

"He was the son of a powerful politician. He managed to bribe some witnesses and threatened the remaining. So no one testified in court."

"But they all identified the murderer initially, when the FIR was filed?"

"Yes,"

"Hmm, was the Judge also influenced to acquit the accused? Surely so many witnesses changing their earlier statements should have alerted the Judge that something was amiss?"

"It should have, but a Judge is bound by the law and evidence."

"Hmm. How long did the trial last?"

"In the Trial Court, about seven years…yes, he was acquitted in early 2006."

"So after a trial of almost seven years, the accused is acquitted, because the court felt the evidence was not enough?!"

"Yes,"

"That's when the protests began?"

"Yes. It was unprecedented. For too long, the public had kind of made a deal with the fact that the rich and powerful committed crimes with impunity. But Jessica Lall case verdict didn't get ignored. Something about the case had stirred a reaction that was never seen before."

"Did people pay attention to this case because the victim was a model?"

"No no, I think not. I think people got serious about the real issues plaguing the justice system in the country because of this case. What enraged people was probably the flimsy reason why the murder took place. The girl had to die simply because she refused to serve him a drink."

"Why did she refuse?"

"The bar was closed per the schedule."

"Oh ok,"

"Initially it was presumed that the accused will get punished. But the actual turn of events shocked everyone."

"Of course! The acquittal of the murderer despite so many powerful witnesses, will be seen as an open challenge to democracy."

"Yes, it was perceived as a personal insult and threat by the people."

"How many witnesses were there?"

"There were hundreds initially and, about thirty two had come forward to testify."

"And they all backed off in court?"

"Yes,"

"That's shocking! If such powerful and influential witnesses, thirty two of them, could be threatened and pressured to remain silent then what might happen to ordinary citizens? I can see why people were angry."

"While many were angry others were scared of the consequences of keeping quiet."

"Hmm,"

"Yes. They would not be consoled by the Judge's technical reasons supporting the acquittal. So people took it seriously and began to protest. There were rallies, marches and candlelight vigils…all held peacefully yet demonstrated people's anguish and determination to take meaningful action."

"How did these massive protests get organized?"

"Mainly through mobile phone messages by youngsters, with some impetus from concerned media persons."

"Hmm,"

"Yes, a few good journalists made the public aware of what had happened and pointed out the need for serious action. People realized that whatever needed to be done had to be done by themselves since the system had failed them,"

"Then what happened?"

"The people succeeded! In…moving the wheels of justice," Anwitha said dramatically and smiled. "The High Court took up the case, tried it on fast track basis,"

"Oh did the High Court reverse the decision?"

"Yes. It imposed life sentence on the accused in December 2006 based on the same evidence."

"Hmm,"

"The High Court also said, the Trial Court should have inquired into the reasons why the witnesses turned hostile,"

"Okay! Impressed. If people are alert and work together, they can get the authorities to act and, modern technology aids in the process!!"

"Absolutely!!"

"Now, what's the latest news about the Jessica Lall case did you read?"

"Oh, the accused had appealed to the Supreme Court against the decision of the High Court. The Supreme Court had reserved its judgment after hearing. The verdict will be pronounced in a couple of days,"

"I'm sure the Supreme Court will do its duty. They cannot fail in a matter when they know the whole country is watching."

"Hmm,"

"So what did you want to tell me?" she said.

"Oh. Yes, there's a small change in plans. I need to go to work for couple of hours tomorrow,"

"But we are leaving to India tomorrow afternoon!"

"Yeah, I know. I'll finish my work and join you at the airport by 12 noon."

"What…bummer."

***

"Hello?" Mia said answering the call.

"Hi, did you get a chance to read my email?" the law clerk said.

"Yes, just did. Guess we have everything we need to initiate the investigation against Peter."

"Okay. But, wait until I find a new job and quit this place."

"Sure, You can be the star witness…sorry, got to go, my baby woke up!"

"No problem."

32. Good Judgment

On April 18th, 2010 Anwitha and Mahesh landed in the new Kempegowda International Airport at Bangalore at 1 a.m. They got out after an hour and spotted their parents waiting to receive them.

"You have lost so much weight!" Anwitha's mom said.

"Have I?"

"Don't worry you will be properly looked after here in the coming weeks," Mahesh said and everyone laughed.

They got into a taxi that maneuvered its way through the traffic. Although Anwitha had driven in India for many years, it took her a few minutes to get comfortable with the way the taxi guy was driving. It is a whole different art to drive in India and requires unique skills. In a way it is simpler. It's all about maneuvering your way through the empty space among the vehicles, and being alert about other vehicles around you competing to take the same spot as you at any given time. There is a general understanding among the drivers about when and how to yield and take your right of way. Everyone will try their very best to not hit you and will most often honor the traffic signals. Sign boards may be honored at the driver's discretion. Having driven in India for so many years, it was hard for Anwitha to adapt to the way of driving in US. Stop signs meant stop, whether or not another vehicle was in sight at the cross roads. In India she would invite a lot of impatient honking if she stopped at a stop sign unless there was also a red light to back it, or a traffic police man signaling to stop. Also, while changing lanes in India, one just moved to the neighboring lane after a cursory examination of the surrounding vehicles. If there was anybody in the blind spot they would honk and let you know, and you simply let them pass before proceeding to change lanes. In US however, one has to turn one's head and check if all the blind spots are clear and safe, before changing lanes quickly. Anwitha would get petrified doing that especially on the freeways in the US, where the average speed would be around seventy to eighty miles an hour. She would fear that in the few intervening seconds between checking the blind spots and changing lanes the situation may have significantly changed.

Everyone fell forward when the taxi came to a sudden stop at a traffic signal.

"Isn't it fun to ride with no seatbelt?!" somebody said.

"Not when you are asleep!" Mahesh said and everyone laughed.

When they finally reached home after the roller coaster ride, it was around 3 a.m. Everyone quickly unloaded the luggage, and got back inside the house to catch up on their sleep.

When she woke up at noon, Anwitha's mother informed her the coming week was booked with visits to relatives all over Bangalore. *"Oh yes, I have to meet my friends as well,"* Anwitha messaged all her friends to let them know she was in town.

Anwitha was sure she would gain a few pounds after eating all those sweets their relatives and friends would make her eat to express their affection. Not that she didn't relish it. Although Indian food was available in plenty in the Bay Area, there was something missing in them. The idlies in India smelt different, the coffee tasted better and the chaat felt authentic.

"Hopefully the jetlag will be gone by tomorrow," she thought, going to sleep that evening. Mahesh seemed to be totally unaffected and had gone out shopping and exploring the same day.

***

Anwitha heard the TV in the living room go, "Life sentence for Manu Sharma in the Jessica Lall murder case, says the Supreme Court of India…the order dated April 19th 2010, ends the matter, upholding the decision of the High Court,"

"Hmm," Anwitha finished her dinner and went to the living room.

The landline phone rang. Anwitha's dad lowered the TV volume and picked up the phone.

"Hello?"

"Here, it is Sharan," he said and gave the phone to Anwitha.

"Hello?!!" Anwitha said.

"Heard you were in town?!!"

"Hey Sharan! How are you?"

"Great! You?"

"Good too!"

"Was a bit busy in Delhi. Had some work in the Supreme Court. Just returned. Got your message yesterday."

"Oh! You are a big shot lawyer now!"

"Ha ha no no, hagenilla, you know what, I just read this decision of the Supreme Court!"

"On Jessica Lall case?!"

"Yes! See what the citizens can achieve if they stay united!" laughed Sharan.

"Yes, I know. That's why I say we do not need jury trial in today's age and time. People can monitor the state easily now, so leave the professional functions to the professionally trained."

"There you go again!"

"Why? Don't you agree?"

"I do, but,"

"What?"

"Jury system helps ordinary citizens to participate in and better understand the judicial process and…develop the skills for democratic self government."

"Yes, but, it comes at a cost and I'm not sure if the benefits outweigh the harm."

"An ideal jury can be a great tool to deliver justice and teach self governance. I guess you haven't watched that movie."

"Which one?"

"It is a classic…"

"Isn't it fiction!?"

"Never mind. So are you still working for the CPLaw Firm?"

"Yes. I do mainly family law…The firm handles criminal cases too. Often I try and observe those proceedings,"

"Hmm, how is Mahesh?"

"Good too," said Anwitha.

"Ok,"

"Both of us are getting royal treatment here. We will both be obese at the end of our vacation,"

"Ha ha, no. You do not get obese if you live in India. Somehow people complain about weight gain and sugar consumption when they go live abroad. Don't worry madko! Simply enjoy your stay here,"

"Of course! I intend to,"

"Hmm,"

"Mathe, how is your work?" she asked.

"Going on. Today I had no court work. Only chamber work. So less tension,"

"Okay,"

"Let's meet before you leave,"

"Yes, definitely!!"

***

Meanwhile, on the other side of the planet-

"Judge Strickland removes himself from Casey Anthony trial after accusations of bias by the defense…"

Peter picked up the TV remote.

"Entire country is following this trial." he increased the volume.

"…Although he denied doing any wrong, the Judge in Casey Anthony case reasoned that since there has been allegation of bias, every denial of defense's motion in the future may invite accusation of bias again and it can affect the trial…"

"And as Lord Chief Justice Hewart said, justice must not only be done but manifestly and undoubtedly seen to be done," Peter set his wine glass down on the coffee table and leaned back on the sofa.

"I need a case like this."

33. Unforeseen

Mahesh and Anwitha went on a shopping spree. It was like they wanted to take India back with them in their suitcase.

"How are we going to fit all of these in our bags?!!" Mahesh said exasperated after looking at all the stuff they had gathered in three weeks. He was a more compulsive shopper than Anwitha.

"I guess we need to buy one more suitcase. You brought only one check in bag. We are allowed two per person," said Anwitha.

"Yeah, that's a good idea! I will go buy one in the evening!"

***

"Just got off a call from my boss. I will have to extend my stay in India and work from Chennai for a couple of months." Mahesh said to Anwitha.

"Oh!"

"The project starts in two days. I will return to US sometime in July."

"But Mahesh, we were supposed to meet so many people in the next two weeks…and then leave together! So not fair."

"I know, sorry not in my hands." Mahesh said.

"Yeah. I know," she sighed. "At least you got this news before you made the journey half way across the world!"

"Yeah, I need to call the airlines to postpone my return journey to US."

"Hmm, Okay," she said.

***

Anwitha and her parents returned home after seeing Mahesh and his parents off at the airport couple of days later.

"Since Mahesh has to be in Chennai till July you are going to have to stay alone in USA. Why don't you extend your holiday a bit too? We would get some extra time to spend with you as well," Anwitha's mother said the next morning.

Anwitha said, "Okay, I will let my boss know, let's see what he says."

"You said he is a nice person."

"Yes, he is."

Anwitha wrote an email.

"Hi Connor,…would it be alright if I extended my leave for a few weeks? Feel like spending some more time with my parents in India. Thanks."

Next day Connor replied, "Sure Anwitha! It will be okay. I do understand it is hard to travel to the other side of the world to see your parents. Pay my regards to your parents as well. Take your time, come back when you are ready."

Anwitha was touched.

"Thanks Connor. I'm really lucky to have a colleague like you," she wrote.

"Me too!" came the reply.

***

Anwitha planned a three week long tour of Karnataka with her parents. They visited many ancient heritage places in Gokarna, Sirsi, Shimoga, Mangalore and Mysore. Anwitha got several souvenirs to gift to her friends in America.

After the tour, she met Sharan and other relatives, and her college friends. They went shopping and Anwitha got a couple of tops for Mia. Sharan helped her pick some traditional Channapattana toys for Gia as well. The same evening she wrote an email to Mia.

"Hi Mia, hope you are doing good. I had a really nice vacation in India and will be leaving next week. Hope to see you and the little one soon!!"

"Can't believe it's the end of June already!" she clicked send and signed out.

***

With only a couple of days left for Anwitha to leave, her mother got busy preparing snacks and sweets for her to take along with her to US.

"I'm making some holige, halwa, and chaklis, they are all dry snacks. So you shouldn't have any problem with the customs," Anwitha heard her mom yell from the kitchen.

"Okay. But just don't make too many. We will not be able to finish all of it. Also, I may not have space in my bags," Anwitha said, packing her clothes in a suitcase.

"No, it is not that many."

The phone rang.

"I got it," her mom said.

"Anwitha, Mahesh is on the phone,"

Anwitha went over, took the phone and said, "Hello,"

"So all set to fly back?" Mahesh said.

"Yes,"

"I'll be there a few days after you reach."

"Hmm,"

"Safe travels and call me when you reach."
"Okay, thanks."

***

Anwitha boarded the plane and settled down in her window seat.

"Hope Gia will like the Channapatna toys I bought for her," she wore the seat belt as the plane began to take off.

"It's voluntary imprisonment for the next several hours!!"

***

Anwitha landed at the SF airport and hailed a taxi. About half hour later she was dropped off at her apartment building. She paid the cab driver and dragged her suitcase into the building and pressed the button for the elevator.

"It's almost 6 p.m." she got into the elevator. *"Took longer this time at the customs,"* she exited the elevator and walked down the hallway.

"Hope there's a stock of instant noodles," she entered the apartment and heard the answering machine beep.

She closed and locked the door from inside, left the suitcase and her purse next to the door and went to the bathroom. She washed her face and picked a towel from the closet, went to the telephone and pressed the button to listen to the messages. The recording played and Anwitha pressed the towel to her face.

"You have one new message, from June 29,"

The message began to play.

"Hi this is Connor…"

"Oh it's from almost a week ago, wonder why Connor didn't email, he knew I was in India at the time," Anwitha went back to put the towel in the bathroom.

When the rest of the message played, she ran back to the phone and frantically pressed the buttons to replay it to make sure she heard it right.

"Hi this is Connor. Mia was arrested and is charged with killing her baby. She is on O.R. release. We are defending her in the case. Call as soon as you get this message."

"What?!!?"

34. Evaluation

Anwitha got into her car and drove to meet Connor. Her mind was flooded with several thoughts and a million questions. All of the memories of Gia since the day she was born flashed through Anwitha's head. *"She is no more?!?"* her eyes welled up. She remembered Gia waving 'aiye' to her the last time she saw her. She took an exit and pulled over to compose herself before getting back on the freeway. In about forty minutes, she was in Connor's office. He was working alone since it was pretty late and everyone had gone home.

"Hi Anwitha, sit down," Connor said as she walked inside.

She sat across him. Her face and eyes were red and swollen.

He smiled at her and asked, "Are you okay?"

"Yes, I'm okay. So, how did it all happen?" she sighed.

"It was a terrible accident. All happened due to change of routine mainly,"

Connor paused and took a deep breath before continuing, "Well, Mia had resumed working from home for a while and Logan usually cooked lunch for Mia and for himself, to take to work, before leaving to work in the mornings. On that day, Logan had to leave early in the middle of cooking. There was a minor earthquake the previous night because of which there was some kind of emergency situation in his workplace."

"Oh, so Mia had to cook lunch,"

"Yes, this disrupted her regular schedule and she had to reschedule the bath time of the baby for that day,"

"Hmm,"

"Later that day, Mia let the baby play in the bath tub with some toys before she prepared to give her the bath. Mia hadn't turned the water on and there was no water in the tub,"

He paused again for a moment.

"Just as she turned the drain switch off, there was a phone call to Mia's landline. She was expecting a client to call that day so went to the living room to answer the call for about ten minutes or so. Then she began to work on her clients' case, as she would usually, per her regular schedule, when the baby would be napping." he pressed his fingers to the forehead.

"She forgot the baby was not in the crib at the time," he said.

"Hmm."

"She remembered about the baby some fifteen minutes later and rushed to the bathroom only to find the baby lying face down in the tub, face immersed in the water and unconscious. There was about six inches of water in the tub…apparently water was leaking into the tub slowly even when the faucet was turned off,"

"Oh!"

"Yes, because of the earthquake. It was usually the sink pipe but unfortunately this time the bath faucet was affected."

"Hmm,"

"Yeah, Mia called 911 immediately. The paramedics who came couldn't revive the baby. The police who had accompanied them arrested her. The prosecution charged her for involuntary manslaughter…"

"Hmm, and she could obtain own recognizance release?"

"Yes, luckily she got the O.R. release."

Anwitha was in disbelief. She had handled many different types of cases before but this was Mia they were discussing!

"But Mia is not a criminal! Why is the prosecution so harsh on her!?! Surely they don't believe she is guilty?!!"

"Well, the case got a lot of media attention in the region and Mr. Peter Williams has political ambitions and probably wants to use all the attention and publicity to his advantage in the upcoming Attorney General elections."

"Oh yes, Mr. Peter Williams the Prosecutor, he also has some score to settle with Mia I guess?"

"Yes. That too. Mia told me about that," said Connor, leaning back in his chair.

"But, what happened to that enquiry against him on misconduct?"

"It's gone into cold storage. An important witness had to leave the country because of some visa issues."

For a moment both were quiet.

Connor said, "I'm concerned the jury may be insensitive toward a lawyer mom. It's hard for some people to believe that lawyers can also be vulnerable to occasional mistakes."

"She was trying to be a good lawyer…attending to her client's needs when this happened."

"Yes, an indigent client, who had limited access to a phone. That's why she rushed to attend the call. But the jury may view it as negligence or…worse."

"Hmm. But, how did Mia forget Gia was in the tub?!"

As if he read her thoughts, Connor said, "Accidents can happen to anyone. Very responsible and good mothers have had this kind of thing happen to them. Remember, Mia thought the baby was safe when she left her alone in the tub. It had no water and the faucet was off."

"Hmm,"

Then he added, "So far everything has been going wrong. The Prosecution has cleverly got the grand jury to indict her. That way they could avoid the preliminary hearing and withhold most of the evidence except the bare minimum!"

"Oh!" Anwitha felt almost defeated.

She asked Connor, "What is your strategy?"

"I need your help to interview Mia and prepare the defense."

"Sure. But, I have never handled a criminal case in California, why would you choose me?"

"Mia has chosen you. She will not speak to anyone. It was Logan who gave me most of the information."

"Hmm," she let out a sigh.

"Okay. I have one more question. Are you going to request jury trial?" she said.

"I don't know yet. There have been many cases where mothers have been convicted by the jury. Some of them were acquitted after filing appeals to higher courts. May be a jury consisting of some mothers would be sympathetic, or may be not. It's possible for women to Judge another woman especially a mother very harshly. Unless they were in similar circumstances…"

"Hmm, this idea of picking exact peers or sympathetic jury members seems very dicey to me," thought Anwitha.

"I really don't know, what do you think?" he asked.

"What are the exact charges against Mia?"

"Involuntary manslaughter due to recklessness, criminal negligence…"

"Hmm, the prosecution will argue about the reasonable person standard…what we need is a reasonable jury who will properly understand and apply the reasonable person standard to decide this case."

"What do you mean?"

"Let's just ask for bench trial."

"Hmm," Connor leaned back in his chair and stared at the ceiling.

Anwitha waited nervously.

"I guess that will be better, if Mia is fine with it."

"Trust me she will be okay with it,"

She remembered Mia's words, *"...I would not want a jury to decide my fate if there ever was a case against me...,"* Anwitha shuddered. *"It actually came true?!"*

"Well then, we'll skip the jury. It will also save us a lot of time," Connor said.

"Okay! Mia is at her home now?"

"I think so."

"I'll drive down to her place and talk to her then."

"No rush. You have had a long flight, must be jet lagged...go home, have dinner, sleep on it and do it tomorrow."

"Hmm."

"Also, better to give sufficient notice to Mia that you are going to meet her regarding the case. So she can prepare as well,"

"I guess you are right Connor."
"Good night, take care."

***

Anwitha went back home and called Mia's phone. It went to voicemail box.

She left a message.

"Hi Mia, this is Anwitha. Just met Connor. Can I come over sometime tomorrow to discuss your case? Please let me know."

Five minutes later she got a text from Mia, "Anytime tomorrow is fine. Thanks".

35: Major Hurdle

As Anwitha drove she mulled over everything Connor had said the previous day and pondered how to do the meeting with Mia. Anwitha was Mia's friend but at this time she was acting as her attorney. Mia needed the attorney in Anwitha a bit more than the friend.

She parked the car in front of Mia's home and waited for a few minutes. She looked at the front door of the house and remembered the last time she was there and played with Gia.

Anwitha got out of her car. She was anxious to meet Mia but felt uncomfortable. She knew it would not be the same Mia. She probably never will be. Anwitha slowly walked to the door and rang the bell. Couple of minutes passed. She lifted her hand to press the door bell again.

Just then the door opened.

"Hi," Mia said.

"Hi Mia," Anwitha smiled and Mia smiled back weakly.

"Come on in."

Anwitha stepped in. They went to the living room and sat on the couch. The house looked and felt different. Unlike her last visit, the house looked very tidy and everything was neatly in their space. But it lacked the joyful energy that was there before. Mia had dark circles under her eyes and they were red and swollen. She looked like she hadn't slept in many days. She was also a lot thinner.

Anwitha said, "How are you doing?" sitting down on the sofa next to Mia.

Mia said, "I'm not okay," and began to sob uncontrollably. Anwitha placed her hand gently on Mia's shoulder to console her and waited quietly.

After a few minutes, Mia wiped her tears and took a deep breath.

Anwitha said, "Okay, let's do what needs to be done now. Let's put an end to the legal mess."

"I don't care, my baby is not coming back anyways," Mia said, sobbing again. "May be I deserve to be punished,"

Anwitha let out a sigh.

"No Mia, you know it was an accident. Please do not give up…think of Logan, your family…all those who care for you and need you…"

Mia was quiet.

"Most importantly, you cannot let that Peter person win!"

Mia looked up. She let out a sigh.

"Okay. Tell me what you need from me," she said.

"Alright, now let's start from the beginning."

***

After about two hours, Anwitha handed Mia a sheet of paper and said, "Here's the list of what I need in addition to the information you just gave me to prepare our defense…send me the details as soon as you can."

"Sure, but…I don't know," Mia said, looking at the list. "My baby died when it was under my care. The jury is not going to believe I was not careless,"

"But a Judge would. They can look beyond their personal biases," said Anwitha.

"Okay."

"Here's what Connor and I plan to do. We will demand bench trial in the matter. Hope it will prevent an unpredictable verdict and will also save time."

"Okay,"

"Do not worry. Stay strong and brave. The prosecution will not be able to show proof beyond all reasonable doubt. We will also be ready with credible evidence to poke holes in their case if at all the need arises."

"Thanks for everything Anwitha."

"No problem. Is your mom visiting you?"

"She did visit last week. but she had to go back. My dad is not well."

"Oh okay."

Anwitha rose and said, "Alright then, I'll leave now. You take care,"

"Wait, can I make you some tea?"

"No, no don't worry about it. I will go back and prepare for the trial."

"Okay,"

***

"Did you find anything?"

"See this."

"Hmm, the Judge is not going to allow it." Peter said, shoving it back in her hands.

"Why?"

"It's a policy paper she wrote a long time ago when she was a J.D. student. As an assignment."

"So?"

"It's not relevant to show culpability,"

The intern was indignant. She said, "But we can have the jury see it. They'll be looking for excitement and will love this kind of stuff!"

"What's the point? The Judge will instruct them to not consider this as a relevant piece of evidence."

"So?! The jury cannot 'unsee' it once they see it!?! They will believe she detested being a mother."

Peter was quiet a moment.

"Show me the document,"

The intern handed him the print out.

He held it up and read the title out loud, "Postponing motherhood-options for career women offered by advancement in science."

"The jury needn't give reasons," he thought. "Hmm, we can take a chance. Keep it in the file," he said.

"Okay,"

"Good job!"

"Thanks, I will go dig for more!"

***

"Will be reaching SFO around noon tomorrow," Mahesh had texted during transit.

"Okay, will be there to pick you up." Anwitha texted back.

***

"How is Mia doing?" Mahesh asked while driving home from the airport.

"At this time she is not doing so good. But, she will be okay," Anwitha said.

"Hmm,"

"The least we can do now is end this nightmare of a legal battle for her. We have decided to waive jury trial. Last week we submitted an application demanding a bench trial by a Judge,"

"Hmm, that should not be a difficult thing to achieve, correct?" asked the engineer.

She contemplated a moment and said, "Yes."

They reached home and Connor called.

"Hi Anwitha, I've got some not so good news,"

"What happened?"

"It's jury trial for Mia. The prosecution did not consent for bench trial."

"What?!"

"Yes."

"But why do we need their consent? Jury trial is a constitutional right of the defendant and it can be waived?!"

"Well, they cited several US Supreme Court cases where it held the defendant has no right to waive the jury trial unless the prosecution consents to it. In fact, in some jurisdictions the prosecution is considered to have an equal right to jury trial."

"Oh, but, what was the reason for the prosecution to deny their consent?"

"Don't know. They didn't give any reason and cited the same cases to show they need not give any reason for denying consent for waiving the jury trial!"

"What ?!!"

"Yes. That is the current position of the law."

"Could…can…we file an interim appeal?"

"We did this morning and it was rejected. 2.1."

"Oh!!"

"The Court of Appeals usually does not entertain piecemeal appeals, but they did hear the matter in this case as we said it would cause irreparable harm if the order is not reversed."

"Hmm, and it was rejected."

"Yes, couldn't find a precedent where jury trial was waived without the approval of the prosecution or the court,"

"I can't believe this. I don't understand…the provision in the constitution says the defendant in a criminal case has the right to jury trial and there is no mention of the word prosecution! They could have said either party in a criminal trial if that's what they meant. 'Not every silence is pregnant…,' says a decision of the US Supreme Court. What about my client's right to choose?"

"I think you have a point there. One dissenting appellate Judge in one of the cases cited by the prosecution has also ruled in our favor. I will send you a copy of both the order of the Court of Appeals and the trial Judge denying the bench trial. Do research and see what can be done."

"Okay. Did you tell Mia about this?"

"No, not yet, I don't know how to break it to her."

"Hmm,"

"She hoped she would get a bench trial."

"Ok, We'll see what we can do. Ask her to be brave."

"Yes."

Anwitha kept the phone down, picked up her laptop, and logged in to her email account. Connor had sent the copies of the court decisions. She took print outs and began to read.

"Everything alright?" asked Mahesh.

"Ah?!" she looked up. Couple seconds later she said, "No. I'm so worried and…tired," she got up and went toward the bathroom. "We'll talk about it later."

"Ok,"

She took a shower and wore her favorite pajamas and felt a bit relaxed.

"I'm sure there's a way out, should find something when I research," she told herself as she dried her hair.

She quickly made beans sabzi and rice while Mahesh helped her with beetroot sambar for lunch.

"Sambar chennagide," she complimented as she tasted. All of his friends demanded him to make sambar whenever they visited them.

"Thanks, so what happened?"

"Well, the court rejected Mia's application for bench trial,"

"Why?"

"The state, I mean the Prosecutor refused to consent for waiver of jury trial."

"For what reasons?"

"No reasons given!"

"Then why did the court allow the state to refuse consent?"

"Because the court is of the opinion the state need not give reasons for refusal when the defendant wants bench trial."

"Well, that doesn't seem fair,"

"I know right? Especially when the defendant has cited sufficient reasons why she wants a bench trial."

"Hmm,"

"Even the appeal was rejected," she became teary eyed and quickly looked down at her plate to conceal them.

"So what are you going to do? File another appeal in State Supreme Court?"

"I don't know yet. Connor says there haven't been any successful interim appeals for demand of bench trial so far, at least to his knowledge."

"Hmm, that means you can't avoid jury trial."

"The outcome of which is unpredictable, based on personal biases of lay persons,"

"Like me!" Mahesh said smiling.

"Would you like judging a case as a jury member?" Anwitha asked.

"It depends. If the case relates to my field then may be, otherwise no. Just as I would not try to fix my computer hardware parts…I can only handle software."

"Hmm,"

"But, why is the state's consent necessary and why it is not required to give reasons for refusing the request for bench trial or anything for that matter?" he asked.

"Well, the US Supreme Court has determined in a case that it is not unconstitutional to condition the defendant's request for waiver of jury trial on the consent of the state or the court. It was also of the opinion that the state need not give reasons for such refusal as it is believed that prosecutors would not demand a jury trial for ignoble purposes."

"But you told me the Prosecutor has personal bias against Mia?"

"Hmm,"

"And also that he would want to win this case at any cost since it is publicized so much,"

"Well yes, but it is going to be very difficult to prove the Prosecutor is biased and overzealous and that those are the reasons for refusing the consent."

"Okay, but what about that principle that justice must be seen to be done?"

Anwitha smiled at him. She said, "Yes. Probably that's a real issue we can raise. I'll do some research now."

"Hmm, good luck!" said Mahesh.

"Thanks! I really need it!" she finished eating, got up and put her plate in the kitchen sink.

She went to the bedroom and began to research. Few minutes later, her phone rang. It was Connor.

"Hello," she said.

"Hi, we have to take a chance and prepare a review petition to the California Supreme Court. Mia wants to plea bargain!"

"What?!!"

"Yeah, she wants to plead guilty and end this matter. She is ready to serve up to ten years of imprisonment!"

36. High Stakes

"Oh no!!"

"Yeah, not surprising. She is just exhausted by what's been happening. The tragedy in her personal life, the media trial surrounding the case, and now this. She hoped to get a bench trial and end the nightmare soon, but it was denied," Connor said.

"Yeah, it is a kind of peine forte et dure," Anwitha said.

"Right! She wants to avoid the uncertainty and torture of a prolonged trial…many defendants succumb to it. I have seen it happen a lot of times in my career,"

"But, we cannot let her do that! I'm getting down to doing my research for the review petition right now. Hope you can convince her to wait until I get back to you on that."

"Yes, I will talk to her. Even if our petition is rejected, better to face a jury trial than to plea bargain."

"Yes, definitely!"

Anwitha hung up the phone and began to work on the review petition. Three hours later she went to the kitchen to make some coffee. Mahesh was jetlagged and was asleep on the couch. She made two cups of coffee and took them along with some kodbale, the little circular fried snack to the living room and set them down on the coffee table and sat on the chair.

She woke him up gently. "It's 6:30 p.m. Want some coffee?"

"Eh? Oh, ok. Let me go freshen up,"

"Yeah,"

Couple of minutes later he was back. "What's up? I heard you go on a rant on the phone,"

"Mia wants to plea bargain. It happens when someone accused of a crime chooses to confess and agree to a lesser punishment rather than contest the case."

Mahesh took a sip of his coffee and said, "But she is a lawyer! Why is she losing heart? She knows the system. She should be patient and wait,"

"Well, she has been through too much! She's a new mother who lost her child!"

"Hmm,"

"She thinks it would be easier to quietly accept a sentence of ten years and serve it than go through a trial that's much publicized. She is also convinced it's not a good case for jury trial because of technical issues involved. And the prosecution did not approve our request for bench trial."

"Why do you think the prosecution wants jury trial?"

"They feel it's easier to convince the jury, or they feel it's not easy for them to convince the bench that Mia is guilty that's why."

"But is it fair to choose between jury or Judge when it suits the result you want? Shouldn't justice be according to law regardless of who decides?"

"Ideally yes, but even when jury members are picked, each side has their own criteria,"

"Oh,"

"During voir dire, persons who are too methodical could be excluded. Some experts say an ideal juror is a middle aged taxi driver! I'm sure cab drivers have their own expertise but in a court case…"

"And, cab drivers are avoided if the case involves cab drivers or driving issues as they would be too knowledgeable in that area?!"

"Probably, depends on which side is doing the selection…"

"Anyways, just finished researching for review petition. I should be able to prepare a final draft before dinner. Just hope Mia doesn't lose hope and give in before this review petition is decided." Anwitha said.

"Hmm, ok, don't worry about dinner. I'll fix something,"

"Thank you."

***

Mahesh made some aloo parathas, raita and rice for dinner.

"It's so good!" Anwitha said.

"Thanks. How is the review petition coming?"

"I just finished it. Have a feeling it is good. I will go tomorrow morning and discuss it with Connor. He may have something to revise or add."

***

Later that night, *they were in the courtroom.*

The Judge asked, "Mr. Connor, these are the charges against your client Mia Williams-Jones…how do you plead?"

Connor rose from his seat. Mia looked at Peter and at the pile of heavy rocks beside his table.

Mia said, "Plead guilty your honor."
Connor said, "Objection your honor!!"
***

Next morning Anwitha went to Connor's office with a print out of the draft review petition. Connor was not in his chair.

"Probably in court," she thought and left the print out on Connor's table with a sticky note for review.

Around two in the afternoon, her phone rang. It was Connor.

"Can you come over to my office?"

"Yes,"

When she walked in to Connor's office, he looked up and smiled.

"Hey Anwitha, here, have a seat."

She sat down.

"Did you hear?"

"What?"

"Peter is appointed as the new Attorney General. The incumbent AG resigned…"

"Oh!"

"Yep," he smiled again.

"Is that good news?"

"No no no. I'm smiling because I just read your draft review petition and the brief. I'm pretty impressed!"

"Oh! Thanks."

"I want you to argue it in the Supreme Court. You will be able to convince the court better on why imposing a jury trial in this case is not fair. You drafted it well and you should argue it yourself."

"Are you sure?"

"Yes,"

"Peter will be there to argue it against me, since he is the AG now,"

"Believe me, your review petition and the brief is strong on merits. You should be able to convince the bench…also, Peter may be lenient…now that his ambition is fulfilled?"

"Hmm, I don't know. I think it would be better if you argued the review petition. I do not have as much experience in California as you do. Also, Peter may use the excuse of 'outsider perspective' to attack me,"

"Well, sometimes an outsider is able to offer a better perspective. Also, Justices pay attention to the merits of what you will be submitting. We have a bar that is very diverse. Your race, national origin, length of residence should not and will not matter before any court. Do not worry about those things. Also, I have demanded for jury trial for many of my clients and have appeared and argued before the jury in several criminal cases over many years. So, it would be harder for me to argue that jury trial is not a good option…"

"Hmm, okay. I hope I don't have to argue on those lines. I want to keep it specific to Mia's case,"

"Yes. You will do it then. Best of luck! I'm pretty confident that you will do well!" he smiled and handed her the papers.

"If you have any questions on the procedure I'm here to help," he said.

"Thanks!"

Anwitha finalized the review petition and handed it to the office clerk to be filed.

***

Later that evening, Anwitha got a text message that the review petition has been granted and the brief has been filed as well.

"Hope the hearing gets scheduled just as fast!" she thought on reading the message.

Mahesh called out to Anwitha from the living room, "Hey Anwi! See what's on TV…!"

Anwitha lowered the flame on the stove and went to the living room. It was one of the news channels.

"…In State vs. Mia Williams-Jones, Supreme Court of California will be hearing a petition filed by the defendant challenging the order of the Trial Court and the Court of Appeals denying a bench trial in the case. We have a panel of experts in our studio, to discuss this new development…"

News anchor asked one of the guests, "Why do you think the defendant wants bench trial in the matter?"

"Well we do not know what their strategy is but sometimes lawyers prefer jury over bench and vice versa. Depends what the case is…"

Another one said, "The concept of 'trial by jury of one's peers' is vague and unachievable. It is the jury of who's peers? Is it the jury of defendant's peers or the plaintiff's or the victim's?"

"If it is a civil case that would be a relevant issue? But in a criminal case it is the defendant's peers not the state's, correct?" said the news anchor.

"Yes, traditionally, but then you have to deal with the question of who is an exact peer? Is it someone who has had similar experience? Similar race, similar gender? Then wouldn't these similarities lead to favorable bias for one party and unfavorable one to another party…?"

DUTY TO DELIBERATE

The news anchor said, "This review petition is from the same case the new Attorney General prosecuted in the Trial Court before his election as the AG…"

Anwitha said, "Oh no! We could very well do without all this unnecessary publicity."

Mahesh said, "Don't stress about things not in your control. Look at it positively. They are supporting your point of view."

"Yes, I know. but, this is too much pressure. Also, now Peter's ego and reputation is at stake. He will not let go now!" she went back to the kitchen.

***

Three weeks later she received a text message that the review petition is scheduled for hearing in September in the Supreme Court of California at San Francisco.

"Okay, these are good omen, it usually takes longer than this," she thought.

37. Review Petition

Anwitha wore black trousers with a white shirt and her black coat she got from India. There was no uniform to appear before the courts in California but a formal dress code was expected. Her coat was versatile and did not seem like a uniform.

She took her case files and stepped out of the apartment.

As she drove to the Supreme Court of California she had a sense of déjà vu. She kept remembering her first argument before the High Court of Karnataka.

After driving for about an hour, when she reached San Francisco's civic center it was 8:30 a.m. She parked her car and looked at the Earl Warren Building in the Ronald M. George State Office Complex at 350 McAllister Street, that housed the head quarters of the Supreme Court of California. She walked into the building, thinking, *"From the highest court of State of*

Karnataka to the highest court in the State of California."

It was quiet since it was still very early and the sound of her footsteps echoed as she walked through the hallway. The courtroom door was partially open. She walked in. There was no one in the courtroom yet, except a staff member of the court. She was organizing her stationary and case files at the counsel table directly in front of the bench where the Justices would sit.

"Good Morning," she said, acknowledging her.

"Good Morning," Anwitha replied.

She sat in the third row and looked around. The courtroom had oak paneling, high skylight and coffered ceiling. There was a large open arc shaped table and seven chairs for the bench and above the bench was a mural of the scenic California landscape. The courtroom exuded an energy and aura similar to what she felt in the court halls of Karnataka High Court.

Her case was scheduled in the afternoon session but she went early in the morning to help ease her anxiety. She had abdicated all other responsibilities for that day and decided to just concentrate on the hearing in

Mia's case. She took a deep breath. Couple of lawyers walked in, followed by Peter and his colleagues. The bailiff also arrived by this time.

Anwitha felt thirsty and stepped out. She saw Peter's intern advancing toward the courtroom. Anwitha turned to smile but she looked away and went inside the courtroom.

"Strange girl. In Tahoe, she seemed friendly," Anwitha thought.

She returned to the courtroom after having some water.

The court was in session and the Justices were seated on the bench in order of seniority, with the Chief Justice Marisol Garcia in the center chair and the most senior associate Justices alternating on each side, starting to the Chief Justice's right. So Justice Carol Ross, Justice Michelle Harris-Smith, Justice James Hastings sat in that order, to the Chief Justice's right and Justice Henry Wells, Justice Gabriel Franco and Justice Teresa Tang-Temple sat in that order, to the Chief Justice's left.

The first case listed in the morning was being heard. The Petitioner's attorney was presenting his arguments. The Justices frequently interrupted the attorney with various questions as they had thoroughly read the legal briefs beforehand. After twenty minutes, the Petitioner's attorney concluded reserving the remaining ten minutes for rebuttal. Peter began his counter arguments. As the new Attorney General he seemed very exuberant in his submissions. His intern seemed quite elated as well. The Chief Justice seemed both equitable and technical, while Justice Carol Ross seemed to go by principles of equity mainly. Justice Henry Wells asked the least number of questions. Justice Gabriel Franco, Justice James Hastings and Justice Teresa Tang-Temple leaned more toward technicality. Justice Michelle Harris-Smith seemed to always have equal number of questions to both parties to a case.

When the third case listed in the morning session was taken up, Anwitha opened her notepad, made some notes and exited the courtroom. She went to the parking lot and ate her semolina upma in the car and began reading through her notes. After ten minutes, she picked up her water bottle and drank some. She got out of the car, took out her files and books. *"Hope everything goes okay,"* she prayed and locked the car.

She went back into the court building, refilled her water bottle and used the restroom. As she washed her hands, she was reminded of Peter's intern who preferred warm water to wash her hands but wanted iced water to drink on a cold winter day in Tahoe. The memory made her smile.

She arrived at the courtroom about twenty minutes early. There were a few people already seated inside. She could tell from their attire and accessories that some of them were law students, law professors and journalists. She knew the news media had got wind about the hearing of the review petition that day and anticipated a huge crowd to gather soon. Connor had told her the courtroom had state-of-the-art technology enabling it to broadcast oral argument sessions throughout the state building to accommodate overflow crowds.

She felt a bit nervous.

"A two Judge division bench is the largest bench before which I have argued so far…now before a seven Justices' bench. How did I let Connor talk me into this,"

Her cell phone vibrated.

"Best of luck!" message from Connor.

"Thanks!!" she texted.

The bench clerk walked in. She smiled at Anwitha and said, "Good afternoon."

"Good afternoon," Anwitha smiled back.

"You have been waiting since morning?"

"Yes, just didn't want to take a chance with my case due to traffic or anything."

"Hmm, Ok,"

"It's my first time arguing in California Supreme Court,"

"Which one is your case?"

Anwitha told her the case number.

"Oh I see, good luck!"

"Thanks!"

Few more court staff walked in and sat at the counsel table. Several lawyers, journalists and members of the public also walked in. They had heard about the case through media coverage and were curious about the case and wanted to watch the proceedings.

Around 1:25 p.m., there was the sounding of the gavel and announcement of the arrival of the Justices by asking everyone to rise and the traditional chant followed as all the seven Justices walked into the courtroom through a separate entrance near the bench and took their respective seats.

Everyone else in the courtroom sat down.

Anwitha turned off her phone and looked at her list of bookmarked judgments.

Powell v. Alabama, 287 U.S. 45 (1932); Gideon v Wainwright, 372 U.S. 335 (1963) United States v. Cronic, 466 U.S. 648 (1984), and…

The Chief Justice said, "Good afternoon. Welcome to oral arguments. The clerk may call the calendar."

Peter was nowhere to be seen.

The clerk called out the case.

"Mia Williams-Jones vs. San Mateo Superior Court…"

Anwitha stood up.

38. Hearing

The clerk handed the case files to each of the Justices.

"Counsel for the appellant-defendant your honor." Anwitha said.

All the Justices acknowledged her.

"Where is the Attorney General?" asked the Chief Justice.

Anwitha heard somebody in the row behind her whisper, "The Attorney General was talking to the media personnel just outside the court…"

Just then, Peter barged in with his team.

"Counsel for the state, real party of interest, your honors, apologize for being late," he said smiling at the Justices.

He and his team of lawyers including the intern sat down at their table.

"Alright, let's hear the matter," said the Chief Justice looking at Anwitha.

Anwitha noted the time on the clock. It was exactly 1:30 p.m.

She said, "I'm appealing against the orders of the San Mateo Superior Court and the Court of Appeals denying my request for a bench trial," she turned a page of her file and continued.

"The US constitution guarantees the right to impartial trial by jury to the defendant and the defendant may waive this right like she can waive other constitutional rights for which the consent of the state is not required…"

The Chief Justice put her hand out indicating to pause.

Anwitha paused.

The Chief Justice said, "Before we decide on whether or not you have the right to choose between the bench or jury trial per the constitution of the United States, would you explain why you do not want jury trial in your case?"

"For several reasons your honor. Firstly, I want, efficient adjudication of my case."

The Chief Justice leaned back and said, "Hmm,"

Anwitha waited a moment.

The Chief Justice said, "Please continue,"

"As a defendant in a criminal case, I'm entitled to efficient adjudication as much as efficient legal representation. The constitution guarantees me an efficient legal representation and the constitution only guarantees 'impartial' trial by jury and not 'efficient' trial by jury as it is not possible to guarantee an 'efficient trial by jury'. However, it is possible to provide an impartial and efficient Judge or a bench. The defendant should not be forced to forego efficient adjudication in order to obtain impartial adjudication alone…"

She looked up at the Justices. Everyone was listening to her intently. She continued.

"Going by the history and birth of the jury system and the intent of the constitution makers, the defendant has the prerogative to choose a jury trial if and only if, she believes that a bench trial would not afford her an impartial trial…and not otherwise. The defendant need not choose jury trial if she believed in the impartiality of the Judge or the bench. The defendant has the right to a trial by a forum that is both an efficient and impartial forum which can only be provided by Judges trained in law. This right for efficient adjudication as a fundamental right is implicit in the constitution for the following reasons," she paused again, to see if the Justices had any questions and turned a page in her brief. She noticed that most of the Justices were making some notes. She proceeded to state,

"Reason one. Lack of efficient legal representation vitiates trial."

Justice Carol Ross nodded.

Anwitha said, "The constitution guarantees to every defendant in a criminal case efficient legal representation. In a host of cases, the United States Supreme Court has held that denial of it amounts to denial of fair trial, and if the defendant cannot afford to hire a lawyer, the state has a duty to provide free and efficient legal representation at its cost."

She turned a page of her brief and continued.

"Explaining what amounts to adequate and efficient legal representation, the courts have said that the attorney representing the defendant in a criminal case should have sufficient qualifications, training and resources in the relevant area of practice. It is not enough if he or she is just licensed to practice. It is not enough if she or he is an attorney but has no sufficient experience in the type of case they are representing the defendant in. I want to cite US vs. Cronic, Powell vs. Alabama, Gideon v Wainwright, in particular, to support my contention…"

The intern got up from her seat and exited the courtroom.

Anwitha continued, "In *Cronic* and *Powell*, the US Supreme Court held that defendants require the "guiding hand" of counsel…which means, attorneys must be qualified and trained to help defendants advocate for their stated interests. The US Supreme Court observed that the defendants known as the "Scottsboro Boys" in Powell vs. Alabama suffered constructive denial of counsel. Because, the trial Judge overseeing the Scottsboro Boys' case appointed a real estate lawyer from Chattanooga, who was not licensed in Alabama and was admittedly unfamiliar with the state's rules of criminal procedure. And because of this there was denial of fair trial."

Just then Peter's intern walked back in and pulled back a chair to sit down.

Anwitha picked up her water bottle and took a sip.

After the intern sat down, she continued, "Now, your honors, in the light of this consistent view of USSC that, efficient legal representation is a fundamental right of a defendant facing criminal trial, not recognizing efficient trial by a trained Judge as a fundamental right and subjecting a defendant to jury trial is like…"

Anwitha looked at the intern and then at the Justices. She said slowly,

"…using warm water to wash hands but, using iced water to drink on a cold day!"

The Chief Justice smiled. Justice Henry Wells raised his eyebrows.

Justice Michelle Harris-Smith said, "Sorry, what's that?"

Anwitha said, "Your honors, providing a well trained attorney with relevant experience to represent and protect a defendant, while at the same time, denying a trained and experienced Judge is like…providing someone with warm water to wash hands to protect them from cold but denying them warm water to drink."

"Hmm, interesting analogy," said Justice Teresa Tang-Temple.

Anwitha continued, "*Cronic*'s necessity of a fair fight requires that the defense attorney have the necessary training and resources to put the prosecution's case to the 'crucible of meaningful adversarial testing.' Otherwise it will lead to constructive denial of counsel. I believe for the same reasons, I want those judging my client's case also to have the necessary training and resources to put my client's case through meaningful judicial analysis. Otherwise it will lead to constructive denial of justice."

She turned a page in her notes.

"Reason two. Federal and State laws strictly regulate the ethical rules and qualifications to practice law in the United States,"

Justice James Hastings made a note.

"The state bars maintain a list of attorneys with public records of disciplinary action, so that the public can verify an attorney's information before hiring them and not be misled into seeking the advice of an inefficient attorney, disbarred attorney or someone who is not qualified as an attorney. Even out-of-state attorneys have limitations placed on them. The main reason for prescribing qualifications and ethical rules for lawyers is to protect the public from harm. However, when paying attention to these tiny, peripheral issues, the jumbo issue, the elephant in the room should not be ignored."

Justice James Hastings nodded his head.

Anwitha paused and said, "If a lay person, who is not qualified to practice law as an attorney is allowed to render a verdict in a case as a jury member, then all these measures to protect the public through law practice regulations would be counterproductive and even pointless…and it would be like I submitted earlier, using warm water for your hands but iced water to drink on a cold day."

That invited a chuckle from Justice Gabriel Franco.

Anwitha felt a bit uneasy as the Justices did not ask her as many questions like they did in the morning session. She took a deep breath and continued.

"Reason three. Various laws regulate qualifications for individuals in various professions."

Peter began to write a note in his file.

"There are various laws to prevent unauthorized practices of various professions other than law as well. There are rules prescribing qualifications for individuals entering and practicing those professions…be it medical, engineering etc., They all have stood the test of fairness and are not held unconstitutional. The objective of all of those laws are inter alia, public safety."

Anwitha paused, referred to her notes and continued, "Reason four. Decision of a case by untrained persons is a gamble and is dangerous,"

Justice Carol Ross leaned back in her chair.

"There are many cases where jurors have given biased verdicts, confused verdicts, have gone against court instructions and given decisions completely disregarding existing laws…no one should be forced to gamble with their life or liberty…when you are sick, it makes sense to submit yourself to a trained doctor than to twelve laymen even if they had best intentions. Similarly a trained Judge is better than twelve laymen to decide my case,"

Anwitha looked at the clock. She decided to wrap up with ten minutes to spare that she could reserve for rebuttal.

She closed her file and said, "Hence I pray that I am allowed to choose trial by a Judge. That is all your honors."

She sat down.

The Justices turned to the prosecution.

The Chief Justice said, "Attorney General Peter Williams, let's hear your arguments."

Peter stood up and said, "Thank you, your honors."

Anwitha sat down, drank some water and opened her notepad.

Peter picked up a copy of the Constitution of the State of California.

39. Counter

"Your honors, the prosecution relies on California constitution, Article 1, section 16, which says, Jury trial can be waived only by the consent of both parties," Peter began to read out the provision.

Justice Teresa Tang-Temple picked up the California constitution and turned to the relevant page.

The Chief Justice asked, "Alright, the appellant defendant has given reasons why she does not want a jury trial. What reasons do you have to reject consent?"

"We need not give reasons your honors, according to US Supreme Court decisions in United States vs. Reyes, 8 F.3d 1379, 1390 (9th Cir. 1993), and Berger vs. United States, 295 U.S. 78, 88, and Singer vs. United States, 380 U.S. 24, 37 (1965), and Patton vs. United States, 281 U.S. 276 (1930)."

"Hmm,"

The Chief Justice leaned back in her chair, letting out a sigh.

Peter continued, "The *Patton* court said, a waiver of jury trial must also be with the consent of the prosecution and the sanction of the court. A refusal by either the prosecution or the court to defendant's request for waiver denies him no right since he then gets what the Constitution guarantees, a jury trial,"

Justice Henry Wells made a note in his file.

Peter said, "In *Berger*, the court observed, that the government attorney in a criminal prosecution is not an ordinary party to a controversy, but a 'servant of the law' with a twofold aim…that guilt shall not escape or innocence suffer. Because of this confidence in the integrity of the federal prosecutor, the rules do not require that the government articulate its reasons for demanding a jury trial at the time it refuses to consent to a defendant's proffered waiver. Nor should we assume that federal prosecutors would demand a jury trial for an ignoble purpose."

Peter's intern handed him another case law. Peter opened it at the book mark and read.

"In *Singer*, the court said, in light of the Constitution's emphasis on jury trial, we find it difficult to understand how the petitioner can submit the bald proposition that to compel a defendant in a criminal case to undergo a jury trial against his will is contrary to his right to a fair trial or to due process. A defendant's only constitutional right concerning the method of trial is to an impartial trial by jury. We find no constitutional impediment to conditioning a waiver of this right on the consent of the prosecuting attorney and the trial Judge when, if either refuses to consent, the result is simply that the defendant is subject to an impartial trial by jury - the very thing that the Constitution guarantees him. The Constitution recognizes an adversary system as the proper method of determining guilt, and the Government, as a litigant, has a legitimate interest in seeing that cases in which it believes a conviction is warranted are tried before the tribunal which the Constitution regards as most likely to produce a fair result."

Anwitha made some notes.

Peter continued, "*Singer* court further said, the ability to waive a constitutional right does not ordinarily carry with it the right to insist upon the opposite of that right. For example, although a defendant can, under some circumstances, waive his constitutional right to a public trial, he has no absolute right to compel a private trial, although he can waive his right to be tried in the state and district where the crime was committed, he cannot in all cases compel transfer of the case to another district, and although he can waive his right to be confronted by the witnesses against him, it has never been seriously suggested that he can thereby compel the government to try the case by stipulation,"

Peter's intern handed him another case law.

He proceeded to say, "In *Reyes*, the court upheld the views in *Berger* and *Singer*, that the waiver of jury trial is subject to the consent of the state and that the state need not give reasons. The court also said in *Reyes*, that any passion, prejudice or bias and public feeling that the defendant feared would jeopardize his right to an impartial trial were specifically addressed and guarded against by the trial Judge during voir dire,"

Closing his file, Peter said, "So, your honors, the fears of bias or passion that the defendant Mia may have in this case can be addressed during voir dire."

He sat down looking smug.

The Chief Justice asked Anwitha, "Do you want to reply to that?"

She said, "Yes your honors," and stood up, picking up her copy of the US constitution.

"My client's waiver of jury trial is not subject to the consent of the state, because, the sixth amendment of the US constitution says,"

She began to read verbatim from the bookmarked page.

"In all criminal prosecutions, the accused shall enjoy the right to a speedy and public trial, by an impartial jury of the state and district wherein the crime shall have been committed, which district shall have been previously ascertained by law, and to be informed of the nature and cause of the accusation; to be confronted with the witnesses against him; to have compulsory process for obtaining witnesses in his favor, and to have the assistance of counsel for his defense."

She looked up at the Justices.

"And, the sixth amendment of the US constitution is applicable to the states through due process clause. The states cannot abridge any right of the citizens guaranteed under the US federal constitution. So, no provision in the California constitution can restrict my rights under the sixth amendment of the US constitution…"

Justice Henry Wells got a bit impatient. "But what have you to say to the decisions of the US Supreme Court cited by the prosecution?" he said.

"I'm coming to that your honors,"

"Now, in the sixth amendment, the framers of the US constitution have used the words 'the accused shall enjoy' and then listed a cluster of rights. Hence, these are rights of the accused and of the accused alone, against the state. The state has no rights under the sixth amendment against the accused. It is not correct to imply that the state also has a right to jury trial under the constitution or that the state has the right to impose a jury trial on the accused. Because, if the framers of the US constitution meant and wanted the prosecutors or the state to have a similar right as the defendant, they would have said 'either party' or included the word 'prosecutor' or other appropriate term."

She turned a page of her notes and continued,

"If it can be implied, for the sake of arguments, that the state can deny a waiver by the accused of his right to jury trial under the sixth amendment even if nothing is expressly stated therein, by the same reasoning it should also be possible to imply that the accused has the right to opt for bench trial although it is not expressly stated therein."

Justice Gabriel Franco, Justice Henry Wells and Justice Carol Ross nodded, while Justice Teresa Tang-Temple shook her head. The Chief Justice smiled.

Anwitha continued, "There are many rights under the constitution meant for the protection of criminally accused that an accused person can waive without the state's consent. The prosecution here argues that there is no right to waive only this one particular right, the right to jury trial without state's consent. This argument of the prosecution has no rationale."

The Chief Justice shook her head.

Anwitha paused.

The Chief Justice said, "Everything you are saying is contradictory to the rulings of the US Supreme Court. All these contentions were taken into consideration in the cases cited by the Attorney General today,"

Anwitha sensed Peter staring at her, with his smug little smile.

Anwitha said, "In none of the US Supreme Court cases cited by the prosecution, the issue of efficient adjudication and lack of legal training by lay jury members was raised as an issue. Hence the USSC has not decided on that issue. And hence none of those decisions are applicable to decide this particular case."

Everyone was silent for a moment. All the Justices jotted something down.

Anwitha continued by reading a portion of the *Berger* judgment. She read, "In *Berger*, the US Supreme Court said, we need not determine in this case whether there might be some circumstances where a defendant's reasons for wanting to be tried by a Judge alone are so compelling that the government's insistence on trial by jury would result in the denial of an impartial trial to the defendant…petitioner gave no reason for wanting to forgo jury trial other than to save time…,"

She looked up at the Justices and said, "In *Berger*, reason cited were to save time. I'm also raising the issue of efficiency of adjudication."

She paused, picked up another judgment of US Supreme Court and continued, "In *Reyes*, the defendant did not raise the argument during the trial that the state was obligated to give explanation to refuse consent. It was done after the trial was over. I have raised this argument at the earliest point in time. And the trial in my case is not over. If this contention is not decided now, it will result in irreparable damage. In *Reyes*, the defendant cited compelling reasons like passion, prejudice and public feeling. I am raising in addition to these, the issue of efficiency of untrained jury members."

The Chief Justice went, "Hmm,"

"Also, as submitted earlier, the decisions of the US Supreme Court on the right to effective legal counsel under the same sixth amendment supports my contentions…I need a trained Judge for the same reasons the US Supreme Court says I need a trained attorney with relevant experience to represent me in a criminal trial."

The Justices nodded and made some more notes.

"Just as there is denial of fair trial by denial of effective legal representation by a trained attorney there is denial of fair trial without effective adjudication by trained Judges. Sixth amendment by implication guarantees both efficient legal representation and efficient and impartial adjudication to an accused in a criminal case. This is only possible by impartial, trained Judges."

Peter looked a bit uncomfortable and nervous.

Anwitha continued, "Also, assuming the right to waive jury trial is subject to the state's consent, the state cannot deny consent without giving appropriate reasons. Because,"

Peter scribbled a note to his assistants.

"If the defendant is required to state satisfactory reasons to obtain bench trial then fairness and equality would require that the prosecution also cite satisfactory reasons for denying bench trial to the defendant and insisting on jury trial. To say that the defendant has to state satisfactory reasons to waive jury trial while the state need not cite reasons to deny consent amounts to inequality."

She put the judgment copy down and said, "Now, there is also no doubt that the rights under the sixth amendment is meant for the protection of the accused. These rights exist because of a history of state's exigencies against the accused in criminal cases. The state may have ignoble purposes and hence the right to jury trial took birth…and was carried to this country by the practitioners and followers of the English common law. It eventually became part of the US constitution. By corollary, it is possible that the state may sometimes have such ignoble purposes in denying bench trial and imposing jury trial also. Hence, the state needs to give valid reasons for denying consent for my request to bench trial. Otherwise, the objective of protection of the accused against the state is defeated."

She paused, referred to her notes and continued, "Your honors, the ability to practice law comes from training, the ability to adjudicate comes from training, and even the ability to avoid prejudice and remain impartial comes from training. It takes training to properly analyze evidence, determine the facts and apply the law. Mere intention to be efficient and impartial is not enough…it is not inherent in every human being. Not everyone can recognize the existence of bias, be aware of bias and disallow it from affecting their thinking. This training happens over many years of law school, during practice of law, during functioning as a Judge. And even after learning and training how to be impartial, you need efficiency in the specific area of law to perform any meaningful role as stated by the USSC, in its judgments in *Cronic* and *Powell* that interpret the right to efficient legal representation…"

She concluded and sat down.

40. Unrelenting

Justice Carol Ross leaned over to the Chief Justice and whispered something.

The Chief Justice nodded and turned to Anwitha and said, "Counselor, you make very compelling arguments against the jury system. But, we need to be cautious about setting wrong precedents. What about the dangers of not having a jury system...can you really compare jury trial with unauthorized practice?"

Anwitha said, "Please allow me to cite a medical malpractice incident in a small town in India...," she told the court about the doctor couple case that reportedly occurred in Manapparai.

All the Justices were amused.

"This actually happened?!?" the Chief Justice asked.

"Yes, a case was filed in the local court," she gave the details of the criminal trial.

Peter looked a little perturbed.

Anwitha said, "The problems posed by the jury system are identical…"

Peter rose and said, "A case from a foreign country cannot be relevant your honors,"

The Chief Justice said, "We shall decide that after we've heard the counsel for the defendant-appellant,"

Peter sat down, perplexed and with disbelief.

Anwitha continued, "Jurors are like untrained doctors performing legal operation on the litigants, taking instructions from trained legal professionals. They may or may not get it right. It is unpredictable and dangerous. Such practices if done in the medical field would be unauthorized practice of medicine and the doctors allowing it to happen can be criminally liable. This is not done in any other profession and should not be done in legal profession especially in cases involving an individual's life and liberty,"

"Your honors," Anwitha looked down a moment and said, "If I cannot be forced to obtain treatment from a quack-doctor, I should also not be compelled to submit myself to untrained jurors,"

"Hmm, alright," the Chief Justice said.

Anwitha waited.

The Justices were quiet for a couple of minutes. The Chief Justice said, "The trial in State vs. Mia Williams-Jones stayed until pronouncement of judgment in the review petition…"

***

The following Monday, the opinion of Supreme Court of California on the review petition was published on the court's website.

Anwitha read the judgment with bated breath.

"The counsel for the defendant-appellant/review petitioner has prayed that the order of the Trial Court dated…be set aside. She argues that if the order is not set aside the defendant will be denied a fair trial and irreparable harm will result. The state, the real party in interest cited the following cases…and opposed the appeal saying that the defendant's request is subject to state's consent. The counsel for the defendant-appellant/review petitioner responded by differentiating the cases before the USSC and the instant case…she mentions a medical malpractice case from India in support of her arguments and also submitted several other grounds like...that were not raised in the cases cited by the prosecution. However, at this time, we do not think it is necessary to decide on the question of whether the defendant can waive her right to jury trial without the consent of the prosecution or court,"

"Hmm....?!"

"She also contends that the prosecution cannot deny consent without giving reasons. We agree and grant the prayer of the defendant-appellant/review petitioner in part."

She put her head down. *"Oh thank god,"*

She continued to read.

"The order of the Trial Court and of the Court of Appeals are set aside and the State is directed to respond with reasons for refusing to consent to defendant's request for waiver of jury trial within seven days...disposed off accordingly."

***

Anwitha called Connor.

"Hello?" he said.

"We won! The state is asked to give reasons for denying consent," she said.

"Wow! Great! Let's see what reasons the prosecution can come up with," he said.

"Yes. I really would like to see that as well,"

"Good job!!"

"Thank you!"

"Alright, see you later."

***

Later that evening-

Anwitha sat in her car after wrapping up her work in the San Mateo Superior Court in Redwood City.

She saw Peter's intern walking toward her and waving "Hi". The intern stopped on reaching her car which was parked next to Anwitha's.

She waved again at Anwitha and said, "Hi". She sat in her car and lowered the window glass.

Anwitha lowered her window glass and said, "Hi."

"You were really good in there the other day," the intern said, smiling.

"Oh, thanks. See you soon at the trial," Anwitha smiled.

"Yes, eventually I will. But we probably will meet in the US Supreme Court prior to that!"

"Oh!?! Okay,"

Anwitha started her car.

"The Attorney General is appealing further against today's order, since the ruling is on constitutional and federal questions I guess?"

"Hmm, yes, it is better to settle these questions once and for all," Anwitha said and drove off.

41. Acquiescence

"Peter has challenged the California Supreme Court order in the US Supreme Court and it has been posted for hearing on Wednesday next," Connor said, holding up the notice from USSC.

"Oh," Anwitha said.

"Supreme Court of USA rarely admits such appeals,"

"Murphy's law…?!"

"Hmm, also because of excessive media coverage of this case and, the issue involved questions on jury trials."

"Oh my god…"

"What?"

"Next Wednesday is Mia's birthday!"

"Oh, hope we get a good order," Connor said.

"Yes, I sure hope so."

"You should argue it this time as well."

"No I can't! I'm not admitted to the USSC bar!!"

"We can get you pro hac vice permission. And, I will accompany you."

"Oh, I'm really not sure I can handle it. It's the US Supreme Court!"

"Trust me! You can and you will! We will fly to Washington D.C. during the weekend."

***

On the day of hearing, Connor and Anwitha promptly arrived at the United States Supreme Court Building located at One First Street NE, Washington D.C., at 9:30 a.m.

The main entrance to the US Supreme Court Building faced the United States Capitol. Climbing the steps leading up to the wide oval plaza, she read the inscription, "Equal Justice Under Law" on the architrave. On either side of the main steps were large marble figures. On the left was a female statue, Contemplation of Justice. On the right was a male statue, the Guardian or Authority of Law. Huge marble columns supported the pediment which had figures on either side, of individuals concerned with the law in a significant way. Connor told her there was a corresponding pediment on the east side as well. The monumental bronze doors at the top, had panels depicting historic scenes in the development of law including the one related to King John sealing the Magna Carta.

They walked through to the Great Hall which was the main corridor and reached the large Court Chamber at the east end of the Great Hall. There were friezes with various sculptures and figures on all sides.

Connor led Anwitha to the right front table and they took their seats next to the lectern. Besides the staff of the Clerk and the Marshall, they were the only two people in there at the time. As they waited, Anwitha looked at USSC's raised bench with nine chairs in front of her, flanked by United States flags on either side.

"This is the highest court of this country," she said to herself.

As a law student, she had visited the Supreme Court of India in New Delhi but hadn't argued any case there. She realized the gravity of the moment and felt goose bumps.

She looked at Connor and then at her brief with Mia's name on it.

"Oh god! Hope I can handle what lies ahead today," she prayed.

***

Peter walked in with his assistants and sat on the left part of the front table.

Promptly at 10 a.m., the entrance of the Justices into the courtroom was announced by the Marshal. Everyone rose at the sound of the gavel. The robed Justices entered the courtroom as the traditional chant was made.

"The Honorable, the Chief Justice and the Associate Justices of the Supreme Court of the United States. Oyez! Oyez! Oyez! All persons having business before the Honorable, the Supreme Court of the United States, are admonished to draw near and give their attention, for the Court is now sitting. God save the United States and this Honorable Court!"

Everyone remained standing until the Justices sat down in their respective seats. Chief Justice Samuel Curtis sat in the center with Justice Carolina Martinez, Justice Myra Stanley, Justice Anthony R. Johnson and Justice Harold Murphy to his left in that order, while Justice John S. Wayne, Justice Joseph Baldwin, Justice Melissa Chase and Justice Noah T. Wilson to his right.

Everybody else in the courtroom sat down.

The Chief Justice acknowledged Peter, who was the counsel for the petitioner, already standing at the lectern. Peter began, "Mr. Chief Justice, and may it please the court…"

The Chief Justice of the US Supreme Court did something similar as the Chief Justice of the California Supreme Court. He interrupted Peter and asked, "Tell me, why do you not want a bench trial?"

Anwitha let out a sigh. Connor couldn't suppress his smile and turned to look at Peter. Peter's brief contained mostly technical arguments about jurisdictional error by the California Court and nothing much on the merits and demerits of bench verses jury trial.

Peter said, "Um, err your honors, this honorable court has said in *Berger*, *Singer* and *Reyes* that the prosecution should be trusted and their intention to refuse consent to waive a jury trial need not accompany reasons…"

"Yes, we are aware of those judgments,"

The Chief Justice said, turning to Peter, "The defendant has raised some very compelling issues and reasons. She alleges that the case is complex and so effective adjudication by untrained jurors may not be possible. She also raises other questions like jury of 'peers' cannot be attained and other grounds…these issues were not looked into by this court in the earlier cases you cited."

Peter said, "The State need not give reasons to deny a waiver of jury trial just as the defendant need not give reasons to insist on jury trial your honors,"

The Chief Justice shook his head and smiled.

Anwitha thought, *"They don't seem to be convinced,"*

Justice Melissa Chase said, "But, you see Mr. Peter Williams, the defendant here is not merely waiving jury trial, but insisting on bench trial with reasons…do you have anything to say to counter those reasons?"

Peter stood silent for a moment. It was almost 10:28 a.m. and the time allotted to him was almost over.

He said, "Pray for the case to be adjourned to the afternoon session, your honors,"

Anwitha was puzzled.

Connor seemed calm and unperturbed.

The Chief Justice said, "Hmm," and turned to Anwitha and said, "Madam, what have you to say about the observations in *Singer* and in *Reyes*…? The constitution of USA recognizes an impartial jury as the appropriate fact finding body. And if you waive your right to jury it does not necessarily mean the opposite of it is guaranteed. Also, there are many rights under the constitution that a citizen cannot waive. And, there is no mention of right to waive trial by jury or the right to a bench trial in the constitution."

"With due respect your honors, there is no mention in the US Constitution that the state has a right to jury trial, which would be the effect if the state is given the right to deny consent to the accused to waive jury trial without giving valid reasons…also, when the constitution guarantees me the right to efficient legal representation, by implication it guarantees me efficient trial and adjudication. The jury even if impartial may not be efficient…"

"Hmmm, we see you made these submissions before the California Supreme Court."

Justice Myra Stanley asked, looking through the file, "I see a mention of this case here, in the order of California Supreme Court about unauthorized medical practice, by a fourteen year old… could you explain that case to us?"

"Yes your honors. It allegedly happened in Manapparai, India, sometime around June 2007. A fourteen year old high school student who never went to medical school performed C-sections on patients under the supervision of his parents who were both doctors…"

Justice Noah T. Wilson asked, "Did the patients survive?"

"Yes your honor. They all did. The boy apparently had performed tens of C- sections since he was thirteen and they were all successful operations,"

"Yet his parents got in trouble huh?" the Chief Justice smiled jokingly.

"Yes. When the authorities got to know, criminal cases were filed against the parents and their licenses were suspended pending enquiry."

"Hmm, of course."

The Chief Justice was quiet a moment and looked at the clock. It was 10:45 a.m. After a few anxious seconds, the Chief Justice said to Peter, "We will hear the case for half hour in the afternoon at 1:00 p.m. as requested by you…the Solicitor General may also be notified to be present on behalf of the US government if they need to express their interests in the matter. Each party shall have ten minutes for arguments."

The next case was called.

***

"What do you think Peter is planning on doing? Why was he asking for time?" Anwitha asked Connor as they walked out of the courtroom.

"I guess he wanted to prepare better and come back with answers to the Justice's questions…? Or come up with some new trick to confuse them."

"Looks like the Justices have made up their minds, what do you think?" asked Anwitha.

"Hard to say, but looks like they have thought a lot about the doctor son case you mentioned and its repercussions."

"Hmm,"

***

They went to the cafeteria in the building premises and had lunch. Later they browsed in the gift shop. Anwitha purchased a few gavel headed pencils that had, "With Liberty and Justice for all- Supreme Court of the United States" inscribed on them. Connor bought a mug that had about two dozen court cases listed on it. Apparently, pouring in a hot beverage would reveal the victor as the losing side vanished!

***

They all reassembled in the courtroom in the afternoon at 1.00 p.m.

The Chief Justice looked at Peter and said, "Yes?"

Peter said, "Your honors, we are ready to give our consent to the waiver of jury trial by the defendant!"

42. A Fair Balance

Anwitha looked at Connor, surprised! He stood calm and smiling.

"Okay," the Chief Justice said.

"That was certainly unexpected!" Anwitha thought.

"Wonder what made him change his mind?!" she whispered leaning toward Connor.

He whispered, "He probably feared the judgment may go against him…he didn't want us to get the credit for creating a new precedent…so gave his consent…"

"Hmm," Anwitha smiled.

"Do you also consent to the demand for bench trial by the defendant?" Justice Anthony R. Johnson asked Peter.

He hesitated a moment and said, "Yes,"

The Justices dictated the order, "State of California, represented by the Attorney General of California, has given their consent to the request of the defendant for a bench trial, hence, the matter is now resolved between the parties and it is disposed off accordingly…"

***

Anwitha and Connor stepped out of the Supreme Court building. Many reporters who were inside the courtroom and watched the proceedings a few minutes ago were already outside and streaming the news live. Connor rang up Mia as they climbed down the steps and put his cell phone on speaker mode. Mia picked up after two rings.

"Hi Connor," she said.

"Did you already hear the good news?"

"Yes, thank you,"

"Happy birthday!"

"Thank you,"

"Anwitha would like to wish you too," Connor held the phone closer to Anwitha.

"Happy birthday Mia!"

"Thank you, um,"

"Tomorrow would be Gia's first birthday…for a while now, we have been working on creating a charitable trust in her name. It becomes operational from tomorrow."

"That's great Mia!"

"Thanks, will send you details tomorrow."

"Ok,"
"Bye now,"
"Bye,"

***

The news broke instantly everywhere. Once again there was discussion of the latest decision of the US Supreme Court throughout the country.

"What is the impact of the recent Supreme Court decision?! Does this mean there would be no jury trials?"

"No. It only means the defendant can choose between jury or bench trial and it is not subject to state's consent."

"It may not be so for all future cases across the country,"

"How so?"

"The Supreme Court did not decide the dispute, it was disposed off because the state agreed to the defendant's demand for a bench trial…so there is no precedent created on the issue,"

***

Connor and Anwitha boarded the flight to return home early the next morning. After two hours of napping, Anwitha browsed the list of movies. One title caught her attention.

"Twelve Angry Men."

She clicked play.

When it was done she mused, *"Hmm, if only we could peek into the jury room in a real deliberation without being intrusive…"*

***

It was around noon when they reached SFO. After a big struggle to avoid the media personnel waiting for them at the airport, they took a taxi home.

Anwitha rang the bell to her apartment. Mahesh had told her he will be working from home that day.

"Congraaaats!!" he opened the door and raised his hand. Anwitha gave a big grin, high fived and walked in.

"I guess I will take today off. I'm so jetlagged," she said.

"Okay,"

She took a shower, wore her pajamas and lit an agarbathi for Ganesha.

"Thank you, for everything," she said.

"I need to go out for something, shall I order for takeout?" Mahesh asked, putting on his shoes.

"No, I will cook lunch for us."

"Okay,"

He picked up the keys, opened the door and said, "You know, since last night, the only discussion on TV is about the bench trial in your case."

"Oh, let me see,"

She switched the television on as Mahesh went out the door.

There was an experts' panel discussing The State of California vs. Mia Williams-Jones.

"…you have to give credence to common wisdom. Can we say that ordinary citizens cannot vote in elections because it is based on their common wisdom…"

"That argument is similar to what Heidy had made at Mia's place," Anwitha thought, sitting down on the sofa.

"…should we do away with the electoral process itself?" a panelist on TV asked everyone present at the studio.

One of the experts said, "Good question. You make a good point but there is a difference. Electing a government is not the same as taking chances in selecting a jury…The leaders need to prove their expertise to people that they are capable of handling the responsibility that come with holding the office…actually, your argument only makes my point stronger…"

Anwitha upped the volume.

"...see, democracy doesn't mean people participation at the cost of efficiency or allowing micromanagement of state function by common people. In a democracy like America, people choose legislators who frame laws and policies. People are not doing it themselves. They are doing it through democratically chosen leaders, who will do it for them, many times based on expert advice."

"Yes, letting an expert or a professional take decisions for people does not amount to undemocratic rule. It is necessary to ensure competent handling of certain matters. It is about striking a balance between democracy and competence. The question is, how much of people's involvement in administration is ideal?"

"Right. Democracy shouldn't come at the cost of efficiency. Nor should efficiency come at the cost of democracy."

"I agree. Excessive people involvement leads to chaos..."

"True, but jury system acts as a check against state exigencies."

"One needs competence to decide that, which comes from...not just common wisdom. Also, in a representative democracy there are other ways for people to check the state's exigencies. Unlike the old times in which the jury system came into being, people now have the power to elect and remove the law makers."

"Yes. People now have a more meaningful role and greater power in framing the laws. Through this power, they can monitor the judiciary as well, because judiciary is bound by the law,"

"Right. Also, now the powers of the government are decentralized and divided between the three branches...legislature, judiciary and executive. People exercise ultimate control on all the branches of the government, through their participation in the legislative process by voting those into power who they think are fit and removing those who are not. This is a good way of affording people their right to govern themselves without compromising on efficiency or competence,"

"Yes, many countries around the world have abolished the jury system either completely or in complex matters, after trying them out. In today's times jury system should be done away with for two reasons. One, it is almost impossible to avoid media influence. Secondly, as we just discussed, we have other, better ways to check state power…"

"That's right," Anwitha thought.

"Absolutely! It is not undemocratic to let qualified experts to govern, so long as people have control over their appointment,"

"Well what if the Judge doesn't do his job very well? It is not as easy to hire and fire a Judge as electing a political representative for a term. However, you can easily choose your jury members?"

"Firstly there is a process in place to select and appoint a Judge. This process ensures a Judge is competent. The requisite qualification to become a Judge is immense! Years of basic education, law school, bar exam, thorough background checks, years of professional experience and training after being selected for Judgeship. These processes take care of the competence issues. Still, if there is a Judge with bias or corruption issues, there is the remedy of appeal to higher courts and even impeachment!"

"Yes, and thanks to modern technology, information is available to people easily and instantly. This will enable people to make informed choices, closely follow what the authorities do and check when they go astray..."

"Yeah, we saw that happen in Jessica Lall case," Anwitha got up and went to the kitchen. She made potato curry, seasoned yogurt, rotis and rice for lunch.

Mahesh arrived by the time she was done and helped set the table. They ate listening to the TV chat.

"...jury system is outdated and has outlived its purpose. In the era of government of peers, jury of peers is redundant..."

"Okay, I'll take a long nap now," Anwitha said after lunch and went to the bedroom.

"Okay, I'll watch this debate," Mahesh said sitting down on the sofa.

Her cell phone on the side table buzzed as she lied down on the bed. Mia had sent a message. It read, "Gia Trust for the innocents," followed by a link to the website.

Anwitha could faintly hear the discussion on TV.

"...Yes, the 'jury' has taken other forms now. It has metamorphosed into the electorate of a nation. There is no need for them to sit in judgment of cases in courts as a routine matter…"

"Yes. that's the word, 'metamorphosis'! At the right time, cast off the previous traits to develop new and more advantageous ones," Anwitha smiled. *"Like the butterfly! Look at nature and learn."*

"…That is oversimplification. And, it is not necessary to cast off everything that is old to obtain something new,"

Anwitha clicked on the link in Mia's message that took her to the Trust's website.

"I agree…"

There was an adorable picture of Gia on the home page. The Trust was set up to raise funds for providing vocational training and other kinds of support to indigent survivors of wrongful conviction.

There was an ad break on TV. Anwitha pulled the comforter over her. Couple minutes later the discussion was back on.

"It is hard to cope with abrupt changes. We should keep the jury system because…"

"Depends on the need of the hour. Some changes can happen gradually while others need to happen abruptly,"

"…"
"…"

Anwitha closed her eyes.

The scenes from the hospital exactly a year ago flashed before her. The picture of the happy little family after the birth of Gia, Mia holding Gia in her arms…

…Logan carefully trying to cut the cord…the baby wailing, "Nooo! I want to keep it!!"

"Don't you want to come to me?!" mommy asked.

The baby said, "Yes!" standing up. She stepped forward but tripped against the cord and fell, again.

"I want to keep my tetherball but I also want to come to you," the baby looked at her mom and cried.

Mommy said, "You cannot get to me unless we take it off sweetie! I know you feel sad to let it go because it was feeding you, it was your toy and part of your life and body for so long. But it's work is done. You now need other things to grow further…it is going to fall off anyways. But the sooner you let it go the better it is for you,"

The baby stared at mommy, slightly convinced. Mommy showed her belly button to the baby. "See?! I do not have it either. Do you want to become like me?!"

The baby nodded, "Yes!!"

"Then let's take it off dear!"

The baby sighed and looked down at the 'tetherball'.

She grabbed at the cord, tugged at it real hard to pull it out, just as the dad yelled, "Wait!! Let me…!"

The cell phone began to ring.

43. Forum Buffet

Anwitha woke up startled. She picked up the phone and said, "Hello,"

"Hey! Congrats,"

"Oh, Sharan!! Thanks! But, how did you know?"

"Quite a task you have achieved. So proud of you!! Gopal uncle told me,"

"Oh! Thanks, but it is not over yet, we still have a trial to defend."

"Hmmm, and you got to choose bench trial."

"Yes!"

"That's a big victory,"

"Yeah...And I think it is time to get rid of the jury system that has long served as...the umbilical cord...to nourish the early embryonic democracy,"

"Ha ha! Funny you put it that way!! This analogy applies better to their ridiculous gun laws probably, but it is a bad idea to do away with the jury system entirely."

"Why?! You say that even after witnessing what was achieved in Jessica Lall case by today's technology and media?!"

"Exactly! What happened in Jessica Lall case and other cases, is why retaining the jury system as an option makes sense. Do you think it is practicable to mobilize an entire nation every time there is a miscarriage of justice like we did in Jessica Lall case?! I don't think so,"

Anwitha was quiet. She could hear the discussion on TV in the living room.

"True, things have evolved. But why should we do away with jury system?! It can stay along with other democratic processes and institutions?!"

"No, it kind of creates conflict to do that. Like…jury nullification. A law made by the people of a country can be effectively nullified by twelve random people judging a case…which is not democratic at all,"

"Anwitha, don't we sometimes self medicate…use home remedies for minor illnesses?" Sharan said.

"Hmm, but," she said.

The TV went, "…Jury nullification can be checked in an appeal,"

"Appeal costs time, energy and money."

"It is but a small price to pay to retain trial by peers as an alternative,"

"It is not wise to impose either the bench trial or the jury trial," there was an ad break.

Sharan said, "Or indulge in DIY projects, allow co-worker representation in departmental inquiries, authorize quasi judicial bodies, mediation, arbitration?"

"Hmm, mayyy be Sharan, better to retain both, if all concerns are addressed…"

"Yes, absolutely! No need to throw the baby along with the bath water! We should reintroduce the jury system in India as well, with certain reforms and restrictions of course, and selectively. Only if the cases are fit for jury trial,"

"In India?! Hmm, I don't know…coz, everyday people's individual culture comes into play, and it's such a diverse culture,"

"True, and culture is a kind of law. Courts acknowledge it in certain circumstances…"

"Yeah, but,"

"Get over your familiarity bias! Jury can decide all cases that need no specialized knowledge. We could, may be set up separate courts for such cases assignable to juries. They can be modeled partly on the Panchayat Courts of old times…"

"Hmm,"

"Could also provide mandatory training to jurors so the duty to deliberate is taken seriously,"

"And they ask the right questions as twelve neutral guys…?"

"Yes, exactly!"

"Hmm,"

"Of course, in complex cases involving hundreds of documents and witnesses, or when the stakes are high, like life and liberty, it would be ideal if there is a choice between the bench and the box…it all depends,"

Anwitha smiled. "The reasons you give are quite persuasive,"

"I would say convincing, your honor!!"

"Ha ha, just stated my opinion Sharan,"

"Hmm. We just need to figure out an ideal way to utilize both options,"

"Yeah, I guess."

"I know regardless of what system we may have, people must always be alert to what's happening around them and fix it when things go wrong."

"Yes, they are the great grand jury."

"Yeah. Janta Janardhan! Citizenry is the almighty."

"Hmm."

"How's Mia doing?"

"She's okay. Sounded cheerful yesterday when I talked to her,"

"Okay, when is the trial?"

"Around September next year."

"Best of luck!"

***

July 4th 2011-

"Casey Anthony trial: Jury begins deliberations."

"It worries me," Anwitha said reading the news.

"Because mother on trial for killing her child?" Mahesh asked.

"Yes,"

"Take a break! Let's go out and watch some fireworks today,"

"Okay, give me ten minutes," Anwitha said, closing her laptop.

***

Next Morning-

"…the jury found Casey Anthony not guilty on all the serious charges. There is significant outcry among the general public that the jury made the wrong decision. Outside the Courthouse, a huge crowd of several hundred people have gathered, they are waving protest signs…they are calling the verdict as 'O.J. Simpson 2'.

Anwitha switched the TV off and went to the kitchen to make some breakfast.

"Here's your tea," she said pouring some in a cup, as Mahesh walked into the living room. She placed a pan on the stove to make dosa.

Mahesh took his tea cup and asked, "Did you see the verdict in Casey Anthony case?"

"Yes,"

She moved her hand over the pan to check if it was hot enough.

"What do you think of it?" he asked.

"People are affected deeply when a small child dies. They are outraged when a parent seems responsible for the death of a child. Just hope the public does not react like this when Mia is acquitted," she said, spreading the dosa batter on the pan.

"You think the decision in Casey Anthony case is wrong?" he asked, taking another sip of his tea.

"Well I don't know. How is anyone supposed to know?" she covered the pan with a lid waiting for the dosa to cook.

"Many legal experts felt there was circumstantial evidence to prove Casey was guilty but I don't know…Jury deliberations happen in utter secrecy and we don't know the reasons supporting their decision. They do not have to reveal the reasons or state what evidence they considered. So, there is no way to know or verify if their conclusions are right," she removed the lid and flipped the dosa over in the pan.

"Justice is certainly not manifestly and undoubtedly seen to be done if the deliberations are secret," said Mahesh. "Would be better if the discussions could be open or recorded or more transparent?"

"Hmm, you have become a semi lawyer now. But, there could be problems with that," Anwitha smiled and lifted the dosa off the pan and served it to him in a plate.

"Here," she gave him the coconut chutney.

"Jury deliberations may need to be secret to enable free and frank opinion sharing by everyday people participating in it," she said, making another dosa on the pan.

He served himself some chutney and said, "Hmm, like the secret ballot."

"Yes, but the downside is you don't get a verifiable verdict."

"And the result will be what's happening in Casey Anthony case."

"Yes. I'm just worried this decision and all the hype around it might adversely impact our trial…they might call it OJ Simpson 3 or Casey Anthony 2 when Mia is acquitted,"

"Relax, may be that is why the public is reacting like this…because they don't know the reasons why Casey was acquitted. Mia is going to have a bench trial right?"

"Yes,"

"When is Mia's trial going to begin?"

"In about two months,"

"Ok,"

"You seem to be optimistic. You just said, 'when Mia will be acquitted'." he said.

"Well yeah, shubh shubh socho, shubh shubh bolo,"

"Yeah, think positive, speak positive."

44. The Trial

A news reporter was broadcasting live in front of the Courthouse in Redwood City, "The bench trial begins today in The State vs. Mia Williams-Jones, before Judge Frank Norton...this case has a new prosecutor as Mr. Peter Williams is now the Attorney General...he may choose to conduct the case himself, if need be..."

Anwitha arrived promptly at the court on the first day of trial. A lot of media personnel had already assembled in court, sitting quietly, observing everything and ready to take notes.

***

The Judge arrived and everyone rose. He sat down in his chair and indicated for the proceedings to begin. Everyone sat down and the Prosecutor made his opening statement to the Judge.

"Your honor, little Gia died on June 29, 2010...when she died, she was under the care of the defendant, her mother. We are going to prove that Gia died because of the recklessness and culpable negligence of the defendant. We are going to prove this beyond all reasonable doubt by documentary as well as testimonial evidence…"

His submissions were to the point and matter of fact. They would be a lot more dramatic if it were a jury trial.

After the Prosecutor was done, Connor made his opening statement. "Your honor, little Gia died and it is tragic. However, Mia cannot be held liable for Gia's death. As Gia's mom, she was trying to do the best she could in the circumstances. If there is anyone most aggrieved by Gia's passing away it is Mia. If there is anyone missing Gia the most in their life, it is Mia. If anyone made the most effort to ensure Gia's safety and well being it was Mia…"

Mia began to sob.

"What happened to Gia is accidental. It was not due to recklessness, negligence or intentional act or omission by Mia. The documentary and testimonial evidence will establish this," Connor concluded and sat down.

Mia quickly composed herself.

The prosecution asked to call its witnesses.

"First prosecution witness…"

The witness walked up and sat in the witness box.

"Can you give us your name?" asked the Prosecutor.

He stated his name.

"What do you do?"

"911 operator. I receive calls for emergency services,"

"Ok. Were you on duty on June 29, 2010?"

"Yes."

"Can you tell the court what happened on that day?"

"Yes. On that day, I received a call from somebody who identified herself as Mia Williams-Jones,"

"What did she say?"

"She said that her baby is not breathing and she tried to give CPR but the baby was not responding."

"What did you do then?"

"I asked for more details."

"And?"

"The lady said…by the way, she was sobbing. She said, that her baby was in the bathtub and she went to another room to attend a call and then, she was distracted by something and forgot about the baby in the tub and after about fifteen minutes she realized about the baby and rushed to the bathroom and found the baby unconscious, with her face down in the water."

"What happened after that?"

"I asked for the address where I could dispatch the paramedics and a police officer according to our rules and regulations. Then I instructed her about what she could do in the mean time to revive the baby."

"Okay."

"That is all your honor," the Prosecutor sat down.

"Any cross examination?" the Judge asked Connor.

Connor rose and said, "Yes, your honor."

He asked the witness, "What time did you receive the call from Mia?"

"Around 12:40 p.m.,"

"The precise time in your records say it was at 12:33 p.m.,"

"Yes. That is correct."

"Okay. That's all your honor,"

Witness was dismissed.

"Next witness Mister…"

After stating the name and oath, the witness was asked, "What do you do?"

"I am a paramedic,"

"Can you tell us what happened on…June 29, 2010?"

"Yes. At 12:35 p.m., we were instructed to go to Redwood City to help revive a baby in distress,"

"Did you go there?"

"Yes. We were at the spot in about ten minutes,"

He looked at Mia and continued, "The lady here opened the door and let us in and took us to the baby. She said she tried doing CPR. When we examined the baby it was too late. The baby had already died."

"What did you do then?"

"We asked the lady how the baby ended up drowning in the bath tub. The lady said she was preparing to give her baby a bath and turned the drain switch off. Just then, there was a call to her landline in a different room and she went to attend the call leaving the baby in the bath tub. After the call she completely forgot about the baby for a while and suddenly remembered about it after about fifteen minutes. When she rushed to the bathroom to check on the baby she found the baby unconscious and her face was submerged in the water…"

"Okay, what happened then?"

"The police officer that accompanied us took the lady in custody for further questioning,"

"Okay,"

"No more questions your honor."

"Any cross examinations?"

"Yes, your honor."

Connor approached the witness and asked, "Didn't Mia also say that when she left the baby in the tub to attend the call, the tub had no water in it and the faucet was turned off?"

"Yes, she did say that."

"That's all your honor."

"Witness dismissed."

"Next witness is Officer…"

The police officer took oath and stated his name.

"Tell us what happened on,"

The police officer pretty much repeated what the paramedic said. Then added that prima facie it appeared that the baby died due to her mother's negligence. Hence he arrested her for further questioning and the baby's body was taken for post mortem.

When it was the turn of the defense to cross examine the witness, Connor asked,

"Officer, when you went to the defendant's residence on 29th June 2010, did you check the bath tub in question?"

"Yes,"

"Was the faucet off?"

"Yes,"

"Was the tub filled with water?"

"No."

"Did you notice any water leaking into the tub?"

"Yes,"

"So, the faucet was off and yet water was leaking in the tub?"

"Yes,"

"Did you independently notice that the water was leaking or did the defendant point it out to you?"

"The defendant showed me that the water was leaking even when the faucet was off."

"How about the drain switch, was it on?"

"Yes."

"It was on?"

"Yes. It was on."

"Did the defendant say that she turned the drain switch back on after realizing the leakage of water into the tub?"

The Officer was quiet.

"Yes," he said.

"Did you or a forensic expert check how much time it took for the tub to get filled with water partially or fully because of the leakage when the drain switch and the faucet were both turned off?"

"Um, No."

"Was the leakage audible?"

"No."

"Thank you,"

Connor said, "That is all, your honor," and walked back to his seat.

"Witness dismissed."

After that the doctor who conducted the postmortem was examined. His testimony corroborated what was stated in the postmortem report. He said the cause of death was drowning and that the baby had drowned in the water for about seven to eight minutes and was dead for ninety minutes when brought to him at 2 p.m.

"Next, Defense witness Mr. Logan Jones."

Logan rose and walked up to the witness box. He sat in the witness box, took oath and stated his name.

Connor rose and walked toward Logan. He asked, "How are you related to the deceased?"

"I'm Gia's dad," he sounded a bit nervous.

Mia looked at him and smiled.

"And how are you related to the accused?"

"I'm her husband," he sounded a bit more relaxed this time.

"Can you tell the court what happened on June 29, 2010?"

"Yes. I was at work and I got a call from Mia around 12:35 p.m. She said that Gia, our baby wasn't breathing and she called 911 and help was on the way. I was shocked. I asked her how and when it happened…She said the baby was playing in the tub for some time and she had to attend to a client's call. She went to answer the landline phone in the living room. But for some reason forgot about the baby after that. Then she realized after about ten to fifteen minutes that the baby was in the tub, and ran to the bathroom and…she found the baby motionless and face down in the water. She said when she had left the baby in the tub there was no water in it and she did not turn the water on when she went to attend the call…"

Logan paused a moment and continued, "…anyways…my wife said she tried to revive the baby but couldn't. So she immediately called 911. After that she began to cry. I told her I was on my way right away."

"Then what happened?"

"I arrived about twenty five minutes later at my house. The paramedics and the police were there. Mia was under arrest and the police were sifting through the bathroom. I guess for evidence of some sort. Few minutes later they took Mia and…Gia's body with them, and left."

"How did the water fill in the bath tub with the faucet turned off?"

"There must have been a slow leakage from the bath faucet,"

"Okay,"

Connor approached and stood close to Logan.

He asked, "Was Mia a good mother according to you?"

Logan was quiet for a moment and said looking at Mia, "Yes. She has been a very good mother,"

Anwitha could tell out of the corner of her eye, that Mia was tearing up.

"Did you notice Mia being negligent towards Gia at any time?"

Anwitha felt Mia's hand gripping hers tightly.

Logan said, "No, never."

"Okay," Connor said, "That is all for now your honor. The witness may be excused subject to be recalled under California evidence code section…,"

The Judge asked the prosecution, "Any cross examination?"

"Yes, your honor," the Prosecutor said.

He walked up to Logan and asked, "Was the defendant not negligent to leave your nine month old daughter in the bath tub unattended?"

Logan said, "There was no water in the tub when…"

"Answer my question specifically Mr. Logan Jones."

"Um, no. Because,"

The Prosecutor interrupted him and said, "Be specific. I need only yes or no answers,"

Logan looked at Connor and Mia. Mia wiped her tears. Connor let out a sigh. He scribbled a note and passed it to Anwitha.

It said, "Need to prepare for further examination".

She nodded "Okay".

"Do you think reasonable parents leave their kids alone in the bath tub," the Prosecutor continued to grill Logan.

"Objection your honor," said Connor.

The Prosecutor turned to look at the defense team.

"That question has to be decided by this court your honor," Connor said.

"Objection sustained," said the Judge.

The Prosecutor asked the next question. "Surely, a nine month old would have tried to save herself and invited attention in the process, how did the defendant not hear any noise?"

"It was around the time Gia napped. Gia probably fell asleep in the tub and, the water filled up…and," Logan teared up.

"Why didn't the defendant skip the baby's bath time that day?"

"Bath time was Gia's favorite part of the day. She enjoyed playing in the water and she napped better after a bath…"

"The defendant should've stuck to her baby's regular schedule…why was she so concerned about cooking her own lunch!?"

"Oh god!" Mia sighed.

Connor said, "Objection your honor! Badgering the witness…"

Logan was too indignant to take the hint. He went, "A mom needs to eat! To do all the things she needs to do! Mia was also a breastfeeding mom. She needed to eat for two!! May be I should've skipped going to work that day!! Or in the least I should've finished cooking before leaving and none of this would've happened. Will you frame me for recklessness too?!..."

Mia, Connor and Anwitha looked at the Judge.

"Objection sustained. The latest question by the prosecution is disallowed and the answer to it is ignored…," the Judge said.

The Prosecutor stood thinking.

"Any more cross examination?"

"No your honor."

"Okay. We will meet after lunch," the Judge rose and left.

Connor said to Anwitha, "We have work in the lunch break. Meet me in ten minutes."

***

"Hello?" the Prosecutor answered the phone.

"This is the Attorney General. In the case of Mia Williams-Jones, no need to produce the policy paper written by her as evidence."

"Oh, the law school assignment?"

"Yes. Will not work in a bench trial. Instead you could..."

"Okay,"

45. Crucial Testimony

Everyone was back in the courtroom for the afternoon session.

The Judge said, "Okay let us continue,"

"We would like to call Mr. Logan Jones for re-examination," Connor said.

Logan came to the witness box.

"You stated earlier that your wife was a good mother. What makes you say so?"

"Because," he looked at Mia and continued, "Her priority was being a good mother. She re-arranged her whole life, to ensure that Gia got the care she deserved. I have seen what her typical day was like ever since the baby was born."

He paused a moment and said, "Taking care of a small baby involves so much work and constant work. We shared some of the chores, but during weekdays, Mia did most of the parenting work, while doing her lawyer work from home."

"Could you elaborate on that?"

"She did all the diaper changing, bathing the baby, putting her to nap, feeding, both during the day and night time, pediatrician visits…just simply giving the baby attention…," he sighed. "And cleaning, most of the cooking, grocery shopping,"

"How did you help?" Connor asked.

"I would help cook lunch in the weekdays before leaving to my work and baby sat some times,"

"Why didn't you cook lunch on the morning of June 29, 2010?"

"That morning I had to leave to work early, in the middle of cooking."

"Why?"

"Due to some emergency situation at my workplace,"

"Okay, how did this affect Mia?"

"Because I left earlier than usual, there was disruption of Mia's daily schedule. Coupled with this was the unforeseen water leakage in the tub. All this led to…," he paused.

"…What happened to Gia was an unfortunate accident," Logan said, looking at Mia.

Connor turned to look at Anwitha and Mia. Mia wiped her tears. Connor needed to ask one more question, which he did, being a seasoned lawyer.

"Per the normal schedule, what was the baby supposed to be doing at 12:30 p.m.?"

"Gia usually napped between 11:30 a.m. ish to 2:00 p.m. ish."

"Thank you! No more questions your honor,"

"Any further cross-examination?" the Judge asked the Prosecutor.

"Yes," the Prosecutor said and asked Logan, "On the day Gia died, was she under the sole care of Mia?"

"Yes."

"Thanks."

"No more questions your honor."

The Prosecutor returned and sat in his seat.

"Witness is excused," the Judge said.

Logan walked off the witness stand looking sad.

"Defense would like to call its next witness your honor."

The Judge nodded.

The clerk announced.

"Next witness for the defense, Mister..."

The witness stated his name and took the oath. Connor asked him, "What is your profession?"

"I'm a plumber."

"Do you know the defendant and her husband Mr. Logan Jones?"

"Yes, I have fixed a couple of plumbing issues for them."

"Can you tell me about those?"

"Yes, the latest one was a leakage in their bath tub faucet. And I fixed it for them on July 3, 2010."

"What kind of a leak was it?"

"It was a quiet leak. Barely noticeable unless the drain switch was off,"

"Ok, what do you think was the cause of the leak,"

"It was because of natural wear and tear made worse because of the earthquake that happened. I had fixed a damaged pipe in their sink about a year before that. This time we put new parts."

"Ok, that is all your honor,"

"Cross examination?" the Judge asked the prosecution.

"Yes your honor,"

The Prosecutor walked closer to the witness box.

"This leak you were talking about, couldn't you hear it if you were in the same room?"

"No,"

"Why not?"

"The leak was along the side of the tub, at the joint of the faucet and barely audible, even if you were in the bathroom. You would not notice it if the water drain was on. You would notice only if the water drain switch was kept off for a while and the tub got filled with some amount of water,"

"Hmm, if the leak was so slow, wouldn't it take quite long for the tub to fill up,"

"Yes, it would take quite a while to fill the tub."

"How long?"

"About forty minutes or so."

"That is all your honor."

"Any re examination?" the Judge asked.

Connor said, "Yes, your honor."

"How long would the leak take to fill the tub by about five to six inches?"

"About fifteen to twenty minutes."

"Okay. That is all your honor,"

Anwitha looked at the Prosecutor. The intern sitting next to him was staring at Mia. She turned away when Anwitha stared back at her.

"Witness dismissed," the Judge said.

"Any more witnesses?" the Judge asked.

"None, your honor."

"Alright. Case posted tomorrow, for final arguments."

***

They all reassembled in court the following day.

The Judge said, "Okay, let us begin the arguments."

The Prosecutor rose from his seat.

46. Final Arguments

The Prosecutor said, "Your honor, the defendant is charged with criminal negligence, recklessness and child endangerment under the California penal code sections...and...,"

He continued, "These laws say, a parent is responsible for the safety of an infant child. Abandoning a child in circumstances where the safety of a child is compromised is a punishable offense even if no injury results. In the instant case, baby Gia died. Gia died because of gross criminal negligence on the part of the defendant, Gia's mother. The mom failed in her duty to keep the baby safe. The defendant has admitted to the paramedics and the police that she left the baby in the bath tub alone and the tub was filled with water..."

Connor and Anwitha exchanged glances.

"It is proven beyond all reasonable doubt that on June 29, 2010 when the defendant had left the nine months old baby Gia alone in a dangerous situation, she was the only adult person in the house and that she hadn't entrusted any other adult to supervise the baby. It is proven beyond all reasonable doubt that the defendant got busy 'working' in the living room, while her baby was drowning in the bath tub. Hence the defendant is guilty as charged. She has failed to do what a reasonably prudent person or parent would do or in this case avoid doing what a reasonably prudent parent would avoid doing…any reasonably prudent person could and should have foreseen the consequences of such actions…The death of the victim was the direct and proximate cause of defendant's actions and omissions…," the Prosecutor sat down, after concluding his long arguments, looking quite satisfied.

Connor stood up and presented the final arguments for the defense.

"Gia's death was an accident. The mental state of the defendant is relevant to establish criminal negligence. The prosecution must show that the defendant failed to perceive or recognize a substantial risk of injury or that the defendant's actions reveal total indifference to the consequences of her actions. It is not mere carelessness or brief forgetfulness. At the time the tragedy happened, Mia did not neglect or abandon her child. She briefly forgot the baby was in the tub. Recklessness is defined as perverse disregard of known risk…"

The Judge nodded.

"…the call records establish there was a call…from an indigent client of the defendant who had very limited access to a telephone and hence Mia chose to not ignore the call,"

The Judge made some notes.

"When Mia left the baby in the tub, she had not turned the water faucet on. She did turn the drain switch on but she didn't know the faucet had begun to leak. When she left Gia in the tub to attend the call, there was no water in the tub. There was no known or appreciable risk of drowning, at least to Mia's knowledge. When Mia left, she did not intend to abandon her baby there, she intended to return after attending a call to her landline phone in the living room. However, she genuinely forgot the baby was in the tub after the phone call because of the habit of attending to regular routine. Mia didn't usually give her baby the bath around that time. The baby would be napping at that time and Mia would be working while the baby napped. Anyone can be a victim of the force of habit…any reasonable person can forget, especially things that are not part of their regular routine…"

Connor drank some water and continued, "Mia is known to be a very responsible person. Anyone who knows her whether it is in their personal or professional capacity vouch for her responsible conduct. The testimony of the witnesses corroborate it,"

The Judge made some notes.

Connor concluded after arguing for almost an hour, "Hence, Gia's death was caused by unforeseen water leakage due to the earthquake. It was an act of god, an accident and Mia should be honorably acquitted of all charges against her."

The prosecution presented their response.

"Gia died several hours after the earthquake…it was not an act of god. It was certainly preventable if the defendant had not been negligent…"

47. Verified Verdict

Media personnel had gathered in large numbers outside the Courthouse ready to broadcast the imminent judgment in the much followed trial.

The courtroom was full as well.

***

The Judge read the operative part of the verdict to the anxious audience present in the court.

"…This court holds the defendant not guilty of the charges of criminal negligence or recklessness, not guilty of the charge of child endangerment…"

Mia hugged Anwitha and wept. Connor patted Mia's shoulder, smiling and a bit teary.

Mia hugged Connor and said, "Thank you," and cried.

***

"The court has found Ms. Mia Williams-Jones not guilty. We are waiting for the written statement supporting the judgment...," Peter turned the TV off.

***

Later that day, the detailed judgment elaborating on the reasons supporting the verdict was made available. It said,

"Issues:

1. Did the child die due to the action and/or omissions of the defendant?

Per California Penal Code sections...and other laws, a parent is primarily responsible for the safety and security of their child. The testimony of the Police Officer, paramedics, Mr. Logan Jones and the 911 call records, reveal that on June 29, 2010, the child was under the sole care of the defendant. The testimony of the witnesses also reveal that the defendant had left the child in the bath tub with no water and went to attend a call in the living room. She spent about ten minutes on the call and forgot about the baby in the tub. Some of these facts are confirmed by documentary evidence. About fifteen minutes later she remembered about the baby and rushed to check. She found the tub filled with water by about 6 inches and noticed the baby's face was submerged in the water and she was unconscious. The defendant tried to revive the baby by performing CPR but the baby was not responsive. The defendant called 911 and reported the incident asking for help.

I conclude that, baby Gia died partly due to the defendant's action of leaving Gia in the bath tub without adult supervision and mainly due to reasons beyond human control or Act of God.

2. Does any defense apply?

The prosecution argued that the defendant being the mother of the victim was primarily responsible for its safety and security and the defendant should not have left her infant child without any adult supervision for as long as she did under the circumstances she did. The prosecution asserts that this revealed negligence on the part of the defendant.

Counsel for the defendant argues that the defense of accidental death applies. I would agree, if the defendant's act or omission causing the death of Gia was not an intentional or negligent act or omission.

3. Did the defendant intentionally abandon the child?

Circumstantial evidence to infer intention are as follows.

The call records of defendant's landline show that on June 29, 2010, there was a call to the defendant's landline number at 12:05 p.m. and the call lasted until 12:20 p.m. The 911 call records show that the defendant called them at 12:33 p.m. The paramedics arrived at defendant's residence at 12:45 p.m. and left at 1:30 p.m. Post mortem records show that the victim had drowned for about 6 to 8 minutes, victim's body was brought for postmortem at 2:00 p.m. and the victim was dead for about 90 minutes when brought for postmortem.

Per the 911 call records and paramedic's witness testimony to which hearsay exceptions like excited utterance, business records etc., apply, show that the defendant genuinely forgot about the baby after the phone call and her leaving the baby alone in the tub was not intentional.

These evidences corroborate the defendant's statements to the 911 operators that she was away from the baby for about 25 minutes and had attended to the phone call to the landline from 12:05 p.m. to 12:20 p.m., the victim died around 12:30 p.m., 911 call was made at 12:33 p.m. These evidences show that the defendant didn't delay in getting help to revive the baby as soon as she realized the baby was in serious danger. She probably remembered the baby around 12:30/12:31 p.m., spent about two minutes trying to revive the baby and immediately called for help. Hence there exists reasonable doubt about the existence of men's rea or criminal intention on the part of the defendant.

So I would answer the above question in the negative. The defendant did not intentionally abandon the child.

4. Did the defendant act recklessly or was criminally negligent?

Recklessness requires perverse disregard of known risk.

The defendant took reasonable care to ensure that the baby was not harmed. Because, although she turned the drain switch off, she took reasonable care and abstained from turning the water faucet on before going to attend the phone call. After the call ended, the defendant proceeded to attend to her other tasks per her regular schedule. The baby in the mean time drowned. However, it was not reasonably foreseeable that the faucet would leak and hence it was not reasonably foreseeable that the baby would drown at the time when the defendant left to answer the phone call.

Also, we cannot view the day in question by isolating it. Per witness testimony, the defendant was a good and responsible mother. The defendant has always been attentive to the baby's needs. But this particular time she forgot about the baby.

Would a reasonable person forget anything anytime? It is probable, and I conclude that it appears to be so in this case. Mr. Logan Jones, the baby's dad, in his testimony said that every day, he helped cook lunch before he left for work. On this particular day, he could not finish making lunch because of some emergency at his workplace. So the defendant finished cooking the half done meal which caused a change in the defendant's regular schedule. She set out to give bath to the baby at a different time in the day than usual. During that time, there was a phone call which disrupted the defendant's attention. After the phone call, per her schedule, the defendant attended to her other works which she did when the baby napped on a regular day. The defendant appears to have genuinely and actually forgotten that the baby was in the tub. Can any reasonable person forget under similar circumstances? I'm NOT sure.

It is important to consider here whether the twenty five minutes of forgetfulness would've resulted in the death of the baby if there was no faucet leakage due to earthquake. It does not appear to be so. So, it is difficult to conclude that forgetting a nine month old baby in the bath tub for twenty five minutes, when there was no water in it and when there was no awareness or anticipation of the faucet leaking water into it, amounts to perverse disregard of any known risk. Hence the defendant was not criminally negligent or reckless.

The defense of accidental death applies.

Conclusion: The defendant is not guilty because the death of the victim was accidental.

The defendant is therefore acquitted of all charges against her. The matter is accordingly disposed off..."

***

The media went berserk with the news of the acquittal. Legal experts discussed the judgment at length.

However, there was not a single protest against the verdict.

DUTY TO DELIBERATE 411

"The Judge has given reasons supporting the decision and hence we get to know and verify whether these reasons are correct,"

"Yes. This is so transparent compared to the jury trial. You get to look into the mind of the Judge deciding the case. Because of all the details and reasons it is easy to see why an argument was rejected, or why a piece of evidence was accepted,"

"Also, we can now examine in the light of the law whether such reasoning is correct or incorrect. This would not have been the case if it were a jury trial…"

"That's right. The Judge has considered every piece of evidence and testimony and has discussed at length the arguments made by counsels on both sides. The judgment is well supported by law and evidence,"

"There is nothing for the prosecution to appeal against," the TV show host said.

"Prosecution generally cannot file an appeal against the order of an acquittal and hence the acquittal has become final," said a legal expert. "Even if they could, the reasons accompanying the verdict shows the order is unimpeachable."

"Does this mean it is the end of jury trials in criminal cases?" asked the host.

"Well no, the defendant is still free to choose jury trial, which is what the constitution guarantees,"

"Okay. But the case has highlighted some drawbacks and deficiencies in the jury system. We need to make those reforms,"

"Yes, it will certainly help if the jury is also required to give a detailed and verifiable verdict, like a Judge."

"Yes, they can record the reasons for their decisions anonymously, just like how they vote during their deliberations,"

"Agree. It would ensure the jury indulges in actual and meaningful deliberations so the jury can be aware of any bias they may have."

"Or of any gaps or inconsistencies in their analysis…"

"Agree…"

The media discussion went on forever.

48. People's Court

Six years later-

"The investigation against former Attorney General Mr. Peter Williams was concluded after he admitted to professional misconduct. He is suspended from practice for five years…," Anwitha turned off the radio in the car and got out.

Her phone began to ring.

"Hi Mia!" Anwitha answered, climbing up the stairs to her apartment.

"Hi! How are you doing?"

"Great! How are you?" Anwitha reached into her purse for her apartment keys.

"How is your little one?"

"She's good. Just dropped her at her friend's birthday party. She is not so little any more, turning four next month,"

"Yeah yeah, I remember, and I have a great present to give her on her birthday!!"

"Okaay!?"Anwitha opened the door and walked into the apartment.

"I have a couple of good news to give you," Mia said.

Anwitha shut the door behind her, took her shoes off and sat on the sofa next to Mahesh who was enjoying his Saturday morning playing a video game.

"Oh! Wait! Let me guess…Your book is getting published!"

"Right! My book is releasing next week!"

"Awesome Mia! Congrats!"

"Thanks! I'm glad it's finally happening after working so hard for four years! Just hope it will be well received,"

"I'm sure it will be! The debate has not died down yet, it's still hot topic."

"Well, great that everyone is deliberating on the pros and cons of the jury system. It's ideal if the people themselves collectively decided on the reforms they want…"

"Right Mia, they are the ultimate court!"

"Hmm. I want to invite you guys to the book launch…"

"Sure! We will be there!"

"Great!! Will be inviting Heidy and Heejin too. It will be a nice reunion after so long,"

"Yes!! Ok, what's the other good news?"

"Aha! That is the more exciting news!"

"I'm listening,"

"Your little big girl is going to have a new friend! We have adopted a little girl!"

"Wow! You adopted a daughter!! Why did you keep this a secret!? Congraaaats!!"

"Thank You!! Well, I wasn't sure for a very long time. Logan and I spent a lot of time thinking about it and, recently we took the decision and just went ahead and did it,"

"You did a great thing! How old is she? We want to meet her!!"

"She is five, she'll be there at the book launch function!"

"Okay! Looking forward to it!!"

"So see you, bye now."

"Bye,"

Anwitha said to Mahesh, "Mia's book is releasing and she has adopted a girl!"

"Yes I know! I just heard you yelling over the phone getting all excited!" he smiled. "Good for her! What title did she finally choose for her book?" he asked.

"Duty to Deliberate-*Justice by chance or by design?*!!"

***

June 2022-

Sharan loaded the luggage in the car, sat in the driver's seat and scrolled on his phone. "Boycott Bollywood continues to trend…"

"Janta Janardhan. Citizenry is at work again,"

"Shall I pack murukkus to snack on the way?!" his wife yelled from the kitchen just as their son ran out and sat in the car.

"Ya, but we are going to Manapparai now anyways!" said Sharan.

"In recent times, citizens around the world have been disappointed by their judiciary. In the US, protests erupted after the SCOTUS expanded gun rights but overturned Roe v Wade...In India, the observations of a Judge of the Supreme Court has triggered a backlash on social media…"

"Okay, let's go," she sat beside him.

He put the phone away and started the car.

"To get to your destination by design, eyes on the road, hands on the steering wheel…"

Soon, they were on the national highway. *"Cruise control works for only so long."*

Duty to Deliberate

Glossary

Definitions & Approximate Contextual Translations

Adhyaksha	Presiding officer, superviser (Sanskrit/Hindi and other languages)
Aloo paratha	Bread stuffed with cooked potato seasoned with spices.
Amma	Way of addressing one's mother. (Kannada and other)
Annexure	Document attached to a file.
Bajjis	Fried snack with lentils/ veggies and spices.
Bengloor traffic Hingene	This is how the traffic (usually) is in Bengaluru (Mix of Kannada and English)
Bindi	Dot on the forehead.
Buddi ilvenayya ?	Don't you have any common sense? (Kannada)
Chaat	Type of fast food
Chaklis	Crunchy fried snack (Kannada)
Channapattana	A town in Karnataka state.
Chennagide	It's good. (Kannada)
Desi	Related to Indian subcontinent.
Dosa or dose	Pan cake(usually of rice/lentil batter)
FIR	First Information Report
Gobi paratha	Bread stuffed with cauliflower/spices
Hagenilla	Nothing of that sort. (Kannada)
Halwa	A sweet dish
Hey Bhagvan!	Oh God! (Hindi and other)
Hinglish	Mix of Hindi and English
Holige,	Type of sweet bread
Houdu	Yes. (Kannada)
Idly	Rice and lentil cake.
Inter alia	Among other things (Latin)
Jhumkas/Jhumki	Type of earrings
Kaju katli	Sweet dish made of cashew nuts
Kasuti	A style of embroidery from Karnataka state.
Kinglish	Mix of Kannada and English
Kodagana koli nungitha	The hen swallowed the monkey (Kannada) -has a deeper metaphorical meaning.
Kurti	Tunic/Top

Mathe?	What else?(Kannada)
Mathenilla	Nothing much (Kannada)
Mava	Uncle(usually mother's brother)
Moong dal	Green gram (lentil)
Murukkus	Crunchy fried snack(Tamil)
Nodu	See, Look (Kannada)
Paithiyama?	Are you insane?(Tamil)
Panchayat	Local self government and judicial body.
Peine forte et dure	Strong and hard punishment. (French)
Prima facie	At first view.(Latin)
Pro bono	Without charge (Latin)
Quasi	Almost, seemingly.
Raita	Yogurt with veggies(raw)
Roti	Flat bread (Hindi and other)
Sabzi	Cooked and seasoned vegetables.
Salwar Kameez	Traditional attire with wide or narrow trousers and tunic.
Sambar	Stew with lentils, vegetables and seasoned spices.
Saree	Long fabric draped by women -a traditional, timeless Indian attire.
Sub judice	Under judicial consideration(Latin)
Tagolli	Please take it/here you are (Kannada)
Toor dal	Split pigeon peas(lentil)
Upma	Seasoned and cooked semolina or vermicelli with veggies.
Yemi idi?	What is this?(Telugu)
Yen ayitu?	What happened? (Kannada)
Yen samachara?	What's up? (Kannada)

About the author-

Kausalya Hegde is a dual licensed attorney with law practice experience in California, USA and India. Born and raised in Karnataka, India, she earned her Bachelor of Laws/LL.B., from Bangalore University Law College, India and her Master of Laws/LL.M., from Santa Clara University School of Law, USA, on moving to USA after marriage.

Apart from writing, she likes music, painting, travelling and meditation.

Thank you for reading my debut book!

Please leave a review online at Amazon / where you got this book. Even a single word of feedback would mean a lot!

Thanks,
Kausalya

www.ingramcontent.com/pod-product-compliance
Lightning Source LLC
Chambersburg PA
CBHW031603210526
45464CB00004B/1417